How to Keep Your Child Safe

Also by Allison Lee

The Parents's Guide to Childcare
How to choose the right childcare for you and your child

Growing Great Kids
*The good parents guide to confident, sociable and
well-behaved children*

Starting Your Own Childminding Business
How to set up good quality childcare in your own home

The Childminder's Companion
A practical guide to looking after other people's children

howtobooks
How To Books Ltd
Spring Hill House
Spring Hill Road
Begbroke, Oxford OX5 1RX
info@howtobooks.co.uk
www.howtobooks.co.uk

How to Keep Your Child Safe

A PARENT'S GUIDE TO PROTECTING THEIR CHILDREN

ALLISON LEE

howtobooks

Published by How To Books Ltd
Spring Hill House
Spring Hill Road
Begbroke, Oxford OX5 1RX, United Kingdom
Tel: (01865) 375794, Fax: (01865) 379162
info@howtobooks.co.uk
www.howtobooks.co.uk

How To Books greatly reduce the carbon footprint of their books by
sourcing their typesetting and printing in the UK.

British Library Cataloguing in Publication Data
A catalogue record for this book is available from the British Library

ISBN 978 1 84528 236 3

Produced for How to Books by Deer Park Productions, Tavistock
Typeset by Pantek Arts Ltd, Maidstone, Kent
Printed and bound by Cromwell Press Ltd, Trowbridge, Wiltshire

NOTE: The material contained in this book is set out in good faith for
general guidance and no liability can be accepted for loss or expense
incurred as a result of relying in particular circumstances on statements
made in this book. Laws and regulations are complex and liable to change,
and readers should check the current position with the relevant authorities
before making personal arrangements.

Contents

Introduction

Is it easy to keep your child safe?

Do you know where your teenager is every hour of every day?

How late do they have to be out until before you start to worry?

Is abduction something you think and worry about regularly?

Do you resist the temptation to allow your child to play on the streets with their friends?

These are just some of the many questions that parents the world over ask themselves on a daily basis. With media coverage of hit and run drivers, child abduction, paedophiles, infant deaths from drowning in garden ponds or choking on food, bullying and suicide; is it any wonder that many parents suffer sleepless nights from time to time, worrying about the safety of their children?

Accidents can happen at any time and to anyone. Complete prevention is impossible. It is, however, paramount that parents eliminate as many possible risks and dangers in order for their children to grow up happy and enjoy the freedom they deserve.

Parents, of course, cannot be completely in control of all the things which affect their child's lives. As a child gets older, they will spend increasing amounts of time away from the home in a world which can be harsh and uncaring. Children also have their own characteristics and personalities which can affect the way they view things and this is something which parents cannot change or control.

However, in a world of violence and crime it is not acceptable for parents to be lax in their duty when keeping children safe and it is essential that they are vigilant at all times. This is difficult. Without wrapping children in cotton wool, how can you reasonably protect them from the dangers that they may encounter on a daily basis? It is important that we all realise that sometimes even the most vigilant of parents can drop their guard for a short time and this is when disaster strikes.

This book will look at a number of issues, some much more common than others. With caution it is possible to protect your child whilst allowing them a certain degree of freedom and giving them the opportunity to take risks and make choices.

Much has to depend on the age and nature of the child in question as even responsible *adults* are not without exception when it comes to danger. Parents are the most important people in a child's life and the ultimate responsibility for their safety must rest with them.

This book is not intended to frighten or criticise today's parents, but merely aims to point out the many different dangers faced by children every day. This book will offer help and advice to eliminate these dangers wherever possible.

As a childcare practitioner, part of my compulsory training involves first aid. As a parent, I would recommend this training to everyone who cares for children. Accidents can happen to anyone at any time, however having the knowledge to deal with an accident or emergency can sometimes mean the difference between life and death.

Acknowledgements

I would like to thank Nikki Read and Giles Lewis of How To Books for allowing me the opportunity of having another of my books published through them.

As a mother and childminder I am very aware of the dangers that children face today. It has been my duty to eliminate as many of these dangers as possible whilst caring, not only for my own children, but also for the children in my childminding setting.

As a child I often despaired of my own parents when they set me a time to come home by and scolded me if I was late. At the time, their behaviour appeared unreasonable. However, once I became a mother myself I began to understand the necessity for looking out for our children in order to keep them safe and prevent accidents. I too have felt the pangs of fear when my own young children have wandered out of sight or tripped over something and fallen.

Although I completely understand that accidents can happen to anyone – that is why they are called 'accidents' – I also realise the importance of eliminating as many potential dangers as possible.

My own children, Sam and David, have, at times, caused me great anxiety and I had hoped that once they hit their teens the worry and fear would evaporate – how wrong I was! The infant dangers have simply been replaced by learning to drive, nights out and internet chat rooms and my sleepless nights remain ongoing!

I would like to thank my husband, Mark, for helping me to keep our own children safe and for his ongoing support and loyalty.

1

Keeping Your Child Safe in the Home

THE DANGERS IN THE HOME

Along with the joys of parenthood come a great deal of worries, not least how to keep our children safe. Whilst most of us worry about our child's safety away from the home or when we are not around, we often forget about the very real dangers inside our own houses. Of course our homes are where we should be able to relax and feel safe and secure however, it is also essential that we remember that our home can also be a place full of hidden danger and hazards, which if not kept in check, have the potential to seriously harm or even kill our children.

It is impossible for parents to eliminate every single danger imaginable. Even the most vigilant of parents, who are aware of where their children are and what they are doing most of the time, will not be able to protect their children 24 hours a day, seven days a week. This is because accidents can happen to anyone at any time. However it is possible to eliminate as many dangers as possible and to be prepared for all eventualities. Always remember that 'prevention is better than the cure' and one of the most important aspects of ensuring children are safe is to supervise them as much as possible.

By their very nature, children are inquisitive and it is their inquisitiveness which can sometimes land them in danger. They love to explore their surroundings and often enjoy playing with things which are 'out of bounds' rather than the toys their parents have bought for them. Some children are accident prone and have absolutely no sense of danger whatsoever, whilst others are more cautious and will actually limit the risks they take. Remember, however, that being able to recognise dangers and limit risks comes about with age and not all children are aware of when and how to practise safe measures.

REDUCING THE RISK OF DANGER

Despite being our shelter and a place to relax, our homes are full of potential dangers to a child. Often even the simplest of everyday appliances can be fraught with danger if a child is allowed the freedom to experiment and explore unsupervised. You can reduce the risk of danger in your home by fitting smoke alarms and carbon monoxide detectors and by checking the batteries regularly – it is pointless having any kind of alarm or detector if the batteries are flat and lifeless!

◆ FACT ◆

One of the main dangers which we all need to be aware of in our homes is carbon monoxide poisoning. Known as the 'silent killer' because it cannot be seen or smelt carbon monoxide can be potentially lethal. Make sure you have your gas boiler and gas appliances serviced regularly by a Corgi registered engineer and ensure that you have a carbon monoxide detector in all rooms where potential fumes may harbour.

KEEPING BABIES SAFE

Babies, despite being unable to move around, are still vulnerable to danger. In fact, they are probably more vulnerable simply because parents wrongly assume that because they are not yet mobile the dangers around the home are of less importance to them. Leaving a baby on the bed because they are unable to sit up or move around may lull a parent into a false sense of security as they may think, wrongly, that their child is not in any danger. But what happens when the child learns to turn over for the first time? If they are on the bed when this happens the chances are they will end up on the floor! Practise safe methods from the very outset and you will help to eliminate these kinds of dangers.

Never leave a baby unattended on a bed, sofa or changing station and immediately you will ensure that dangers from falls in this way are eliminated.

OBVIOUS AND NOT SO OBVIOUS DANGERS

Dangers, unless obvious, are often overlooked and this is when children are more at risk. This chapter will look closely at each room in the house and explore the potential dangers from a baby, toddler and young child's perspective before offering advice on how to eliminate the potential dangers.

Look carefully around your house and try to spot as many potential dangers as you can. Ask yourself how these dangers may affect your child and how you can eliminate them. Now carry out this task again only this time drop to your knees and crawl around each room. This will enable you to look at things very differently – through the eyes of a child. By studying each room in your house at a child's level you will be able to see instantly if flexes or sharp corners pose a danger.

CHILD PROOFING YOUR HOME

Child proofing your home is all a matter of preference. Whilst some new parents spend a small fortune on fancy gadgets, locks and gates to ensure that their home is as safe as it possibly can be, others may find this completely unnecessary or indeed may be unable to afford these expensive items. Broadly speaking, with the most basic of safety equipment in place – such as a secure fire guard and safety gates – *together* with constant supervision there is probably little need for locks on every drawer or cupboard, safety film on every window or protectors on every conceivable corner of furniture in your home. Basic common sense and supervision of young children at all times is the key factor in keeping children safe in the home.

We will now take a look at each room in the house and establish some of the potential hazards they pose to babies and young children. Some of these hazards will be obvious whilst others can often be overlooked. All of the hazards need to be considered carefully and, should your own particular home need attention to any area you should make sure this is done as a matter of priority. Never put off addressing a potential hazard. Accidents can happen to anyone at any time but with safety measures in place and a common sense approach to eliminating dangers, accidents can and should be kept to a minimum.

Kitchen

The kitchen is probably the most dangerous room of all. It is a minefield of potential hazards and young children should never be allowed to play or have access to this room without supervision.

The dangers in this room are both obvious and numerous. Every house will of course be different but most will include similar appliances and equipment. Each should be looked at separately in order to ascertain how they pose a threat of danger to young children and how this threat can be reduced.

Appliances

Ovens and hobs
Keep oven doors shut at all times and ensure that children cannot touch the oven door when it is hot or reach the hob. Turn pan handles away from the edge of the hob to avoid children reaching up and pulling hot pans onto themselves.

Electrical appliances
Fridges, freezers, washing machines and tumble driers and dish-washers should have their doors closed tightly when not in use. If possible, fit a door lock. Never allow your child to play with these appliances even when they are not in use.

Chest freezers pose a great danger to young children who have been known to climb inside and become locked in. Even freezers which are no longer in use and are not plugged in provide another great place for young children to hide. Once inside if the door shuts the child is at great danger from suffocation. If you do have a chest freezer, whether it is in use or not, fit a child lock and be safe.

Small electrical appliances
Kettles should be pushed to the back of the work surface. You must ensure that flexes are out of reach and cannot pose a danger by dangling near the edge of work surfaces or kitchen units. If possible opt for a cordless kettle that is completely detached from the flex when lifted, as this will avoid pulling on flexes and splashing boiling water from the spout. Microwaves, irons and toasters should be stored out of the reach of children and the flexes to these electrical appliances must not be accessible to them.

Overloaded sockets can start a fire. If you do need to use an extension lead or adapter, avoid cables on a reel as these can become overheated.

Other kitchen hazards

Hot drinks
Hot beverages can severely scald a child, scarring them for life. Never leave cups of tea or coffee within reach of a child. Always place hot beverages high up out of reach and avoid placing on coffee tables or near the edge of tables and work surfaces.

Hot food
As with hot drinks, never leave pans or plates of hot food close to the edge of kitchen units, work surfaces or tables.

◆ FACT ◆
Hot drinks are the main cause of scalds among children under the age of 5 years old – keep them out of a child's reach! Never pass a hot drink to someone over a child who may be playing on the floor. Splashes and spills can burn!

Cleaning materials
All cleaning materials and medicines should be kept either in a locked cupboard or in a cupboard out of the reach of children. Always store cleaning materials and medicines in their original containers. Whenever possible, opt for childproof bottles and containers but bear in mind that these can never be completely 100% safe. Many manufacturers are adding Bitrex to cleaning materials. Bitrex is the most bitter substance ever discovered and by adding this it should deter children from swallowing potentially harmful chemicals. If medicines are stored in a fridge make sure that you fit a lock.

Alcohol
Alcohol must be stored out of the reach of children or in a locked cupboard. If it is stored in the fridge make sure that you fit a lock.

Plastic bags
All plastic bags and wrappings should be stored out of the reach of children. Remember young children and babies can suffocate on them.

Knives
All knives and sharp objects should be stored out of the reach of children, preferably in a secure cupboard. Never store knives on a work surface or leave them lying around after cooking or preparing food. When placing knives in a dishwasher, always place them 'point down' to avoid serious injury should a child trip and fall.

> ### ◆ TIP ◆
>
> Make sure that you supervise babies and children at all times whilst they are in the kitchen. Access to this area should be restricted with the use of a safety gate to prevent young children from wandering in unnoticed. It is not advisable to allow young children to play in the kitchen area whilst an adult is cooking as accidents often occur when adults trip over toys or even the child!

Remember, young children see all kinds of possibilities for play through everyday objects and appliances. A microwave is a wonderful place for hiding a favourite toy. Likewise a tumble drier can easily accommodate a toddler. Both have the potential to end in disaster.

> ### ◆ TIP ◆
>
> It is a good idea to plan your day as much as possible around your child. Housework should be organized so that potentially dangerous tasks such as ironing are saved until your toddler is taking his nap or has gone to bed at the end of the day. Simple tasks such as dusting can easily be done whilst your child is playing. Many young children love helping so involve your child where necessary – this makes it much easier to keep an eye on them whilst you are carrying out the housework.

Living room or play room

Ornaments and knick-knacks

Although many parents are of the opinion that homes should not be devoid of ornaments just because there are children present and they believe that children need to learn not to touch breakables, it is also important to bear in mind that ornaments and other small decorative items may pose a threat to the safety of a small child. Breakages aside, small ornaments which can be inserted in the nose and ears should be placed well away from a child's reach.

Floor space

Children love to make a mess and tidying up is not usually one of their best attributes! Whenever possible try to keep your floor space as clutter-free as possible in order to avoid accidents. Encourage older children to put something away before being allowed to get another toy out in order to minimise the risk of tripping and falling over objects.

Storage

Storage can often cause a problem for families with young children as they inevitably seem to attract more and more clutter due to toys and equipment. Think carefully about the kind of storage you need and if you are considering shelving make sure that this is securely fastened to the wall. Also make sure that children are not allowed to climb on them. Children's toys should not be stored high up but should be easily accessible to them.

Plants

Some house plants are poisonous and you should be careful when selecting which plants to have around the house. Always keep plants out of the reach of young children.

Cigarettes

If you are a smoker you will of course have cigarettes and lighters or matches in your home and you must keep these out of the sight and reach of children at all times. Remember that young children imitate adults so, if possible, avoid smoking in front of your children as this will reduce the possibility of them wanting to try the habit for themselves; or of them being subjected to passive smoking which is, of course, very harmful.

Fires

Fires are one of the most dangerous appliances in your home. Not only can they burn an inquisitive child they can ignite toys, clothing, paper, books etc. if these objects are placed close by. It is essential that a firmly fixed fireguard is in place around the *whole* of the fireplace at all times.

It only takes a few seconds for a toddler to trip and fall or run over to a hot fire – your watchfulness is your child's best defence.

Your home must be fitted with smoke alarms and you must check these regularly. It is also important that you have a fire blanket and a fire extinguisher in your home and that you know how and when to use them.

◆ TIP ◆

Although fire drills are often associated with schools and places of work have you ever thought how you would deal with a fire in your home? How would you ensure that everyone in the house got safely outside in the event of a fire? Would things need to be done differently at night when everyone is in bed? Can you get through a number of windows in your house if the exits are blocked?

It is a good idea to practise a fire drill with your children periodically and ensure that all children who are old enough to understand are taught an effective evacuation procedure which they should follow in the event of an emergency. Think carefully about where you keep your door keys when you go to bed. The last thing you need to be doing in the event of a fire is to be blindly searching for them!

TVs, video/DVD players

Always ensure that the flexes to all electrical equipment such as televisions, video/DVD players, computers, CD players etc. are not left trailing and that these appliances are out of the reach of children. In the case of video recorders consider fitting a guard to prevent a child from inserting objects into the recorder, apart from prolonging the life span of your video recorder this will prevent small fingers from becoming trapped.

Toys
Check toys and equipment regularly for broken pieces, missing parts or sharp edges and ensure that items are either repaired or replaced as necessary. Always store toys so that they are easily accessed by your child and ensure that your child will not be tempted to climb in order to reach toys and equipment. Make sure all your child's toys conform to British Standards.

Dining room

Tables
Ensure that objects placed on the tables are not near the edge and can be pulled on top of an inquisitive child. Never let table cloths hang over the edge of a table as young children can grab them and pull objects onto themselves from on top of the table.

Seating
Ensure that all children, whatever their size, can sit safely and comfortably at the table using either highchairs or booster seats fitted with the appropriate restraints. Take care if using seats which are 'clamped' on to the side of the table as these can often become unsteady and tip over the table. Always be aware of the manufacturer's user guidelines and make sure the child is not too heavy to safely use this type of seat.

Cutlery
Children should be taught how to use cutlery correctly as soon as they are old enough to understand. All children should be given cutlery of an appropriate size.

Bottles
Never leave a baby propped up with a feeding bottle as this poses a choking hazard.

Young children can choke very easily. Always make sure that they are seated correctly at a table when eating and drinking and never allow them to walk around the house with food or drinks. Apart from the risk of choking, children can easily fall when wandering around or playing and if they did so whilst drinking from a cup the chances of them losing teeth or splitting open their mouths are much higher.

Bedrooms

Pillows

Pillows should not be used for children under eighteen months of age.

Beds/cots

Beds and cots, together with their mattresses must conform to legal requirements. When considering using bed guards – remember that some children may consider these as climbing frames and as such they may pose more dangers than they solve! Bunk beds should be used with caution and young children must never be placed on the top bunk. Take care with bedding and drapes around bunk beds which may pose a threat of strangulation.

Avoid putting soft toys into a baby's cot as these cause suffocation.

Remember children love to climb. Never place beds or other items of furniture near windows which may enable a child to climb onto a sill and risk falling.

Bathroom and toilet

Water

Hot water should not exceed 54°C. If running a bath or sink of water for washing, always turn on the cold tap first and test the water temperature before allowing a child to use it. Never leave a baby or young child unattended in a bath not even for a few seconds. If the telephone or doorbell rings whilst you are bathing your child, either ignore it or wrap your child in a towel and take them with you – *never* leave the child alone!

Baths
Always use a rubber mat or slip resistant stickers in the bath tub.

Medicines
Medicines should be stored in a locked cabinet out of the reach of children. Carefully dispose of any unused or out-of-date medicines.

Cleaning materials
All cleaning materials, air fresheners and disinfectants should be stored in their original packaging and out of the reach of children.

Supervision
Young children should be supervized when using the bathroom or toilet. It is important, however, that you are conscious of the ages and needs of the children and respect their privacy. Never leave a baby or young child unattended in the bath.

◆ TIP ◆

Although most people will recognize the dangers posed by medicines and pills have you ever thought how lethal other objects often found in the bathroom may be to young children? A razor or aerosol in the wrong hands can have disastrous results.

Hall, stairs and landings

Gates
I would always advise the use of gates which open rather than the ones which are fixed in place and need to be stepped over. These are potentially dangerous particularly if placed at the top of a flight of stairs and you are carrying a small child. Gates should be fixed firmly in place at both the top and the bottom of each flight of stairs any young children have access to.

Stairs

Many falls take place on the stairs. Never allow your child to play on the stairs and teach them to go up and come down sensibly and safely. They should be adequately supervised until they are competent to do this on their own. Stairs should be void of any clutter.

Banisters

Make sure that your banisters and balustrades are strong and that children are not allowed to climb on or swing from them.

Carpets

Replace any frayed, worn or loose carpets.

Rugs

Ensure that any rugs are securely fastened down to prevent slipping or tripping, particularly if your hall surface is covered with wood, laminate, linoleum or tiles.

Windows

Never place objects or items of furniture under windows which may allow a child to climb on them.

Lighting

Ensure that your hall and stairs are well lit at all times.

Recommended safety devices

Below is a list of safety devices which you may like to consider purchasing in order to assist you in keeping your child safe whilst at home.

- ◆ **Safety gates** – a must for any home with babies and toddlers. These are great for preventing falls down stairs and for keeping children out of certain rooms, such as the kitchen, or away from potential hazards. As mentioned previously, it is recommended that gates which open to allow someone through are fitted rather than the type which have to be stepped over.

- **Window locks** – useful for securing the windows in a child's room. If you do need to open the window for ventilation make sure you choose a window which is high up. Glass film and guards are also worth considering for patio and balcony doors.

- **Corner and edge bumpers** – coffee tables and other occasional furniture are notoriously dangerous as these items usually have sharp corners which are at eye level of a young child. Fitting corner bumpers will help to prevent serious injuries from falls or bumps.

- **Safety locks** – these are ideal for preventing access to fridges, freezers, medicine cabinets or drawers where knives etc. are stored.

- **Door stops** – these can prevent small fingers and hands from being trapped in doors.

FOOD SAFETY

It is essential that you are aware of how to cook and store food correctly so that it does not pose a threat of food poisoning to your child. Babies and young children are particularly prone to food poisoning and a high standard of personal hygiene must be practised at all times in order to eliminate any risk. Always remember that, as a parent, you are your child's first teacher and the practices you follow will inevitably be copied by your child. Children like to imitate adults and, by setting a good example for them to follow, you will be setting them up for life with regard to personal hygiene.

Shopping for food

Although as a parent you have a responsibility to your child to purchase healthy, nutritional food in order for them to receive a quality, balanced diet, it is also your duty to ensure that the food that you do purchase is of good quality and that it is handled, stored, prepared and cooked appropriately.

Rules for food shopping

When you are shopping for food stick to these important rules:

◆ Always check food for the 'sell by' or 'best before' dates. Never buy inferior quality foods which have surpassed these dates. If you have already purchased food and not consumed it within these dates, then it is better to throw it away rather than risk infection.

◆ Never buy cans which are dented or swollen.

◆ Never buy food which has soiled packaging.

◆ Never buy food which has 'leaked' from the packaging.

◆ Never buy food that has packaging which appears to have been tampered with as this may indicate that the goods have been re-packaged to avoid 'sell by' or 'use by' dates.

◆ If frozen food is not solid to the touch do not buy it.

◆ If the packaging on frozen food is soiled, do not buy it as this may indicate that the food has thawed out and been re-frozen.

◆ Check the 'load line' and temperature of fridges and freezers in store. If they do not appear cold enough or if food is stacked above the 'load line' do not purchase food from them.

◆ Make sure that you purchase frozen or refrigerated foods last and take them home immediately. Never leave them in your car to get warm whilst shopping for other items and, if possible, try to arrange for delivery from the store directly to your house as the food is kept frozen and refrigerated en route.

Food storage

It is absolutely essential that you are aware of how to store and pre-pare food safely if you are to avoid contamination and infection.

Rules for food storage

You can ensure the safety of your child by following these simple rules:

◆ Make sure that your refrigerator is set no higher than 5°C – use a thermometer if you are unsure.

◆ Make sure that your freezer is set at -18°C.

◆ Always cover any food which is left out, to avoid the spread of bacteria and eliminate the risk from flies etc.

◆ Never re-freeze food which has been allowed to thaw out.

◆ Never overfill your refrigerator – air must be able to circulate round the refrigerator in order for the correct temperature to be maintained.

◆ Once you have opened a can of food or fruit juice, transfer any leftovers to a leak-proof container before storing in the refrigerator. It is worth remembering that once a can has been opened and air has been introduced the contents can be affected.

◆ Cans, dried foods and packets should be stored in a cool dry place.

◆ Always take note of the 'sell by' and 'use by' dates. Often people think that canned food has an unlimited shelf life – this is not true. The contents of cans should be consumed within twelve months of purchase before the expiry date on the label otherwise they should be thrown away.

◆ Soft fruit, vegetables and salads should be stored in the refrigerator. If you have to leave fruit in a fruit bowl or vegetables in a rack make sure these cannot be contaminated by flies or animals.

◆ Take care when storing food in the refrigerator. Remember raw meats can drip blood and juices – which invariably contain harmful bacteria – onto other foods and so must never be stored on the top shelves. Always place food items that leak in a suitable container and store in the bottom of the refrigerator. Never store raw and cooked foods next to one another.

Food preparation

Children love to help to prepare meals and snacks and baking sessions are an excellent learning opportunity for children. However, if you and your child do not stick to safe practices when preparing food, then the result could be food poisoning. Use your baking sessions to teach your child the importance of handling, storing and preparing food correctly so that they will learn these important points along with learning how to cook. Practising good hygiene methods in this way from an early age will set children up for life and they will follow what you have taught them automatically.

Let your child see you wash your hands thoroughly before handling or eating food and encourage them to do the same – remember it takes no less than 30 seconds to wash hands effectively. (See hand washing on page 18.)

Children should be supervised at all times when preparing food and you should use your common sense – based on the age and ability of your child – before deciding which tools and appliances they are allowed to use.

Rules for food preparation

Always make sure you follow these good practices in food preparation:

◆ Use different boards to chop vegetables, slice bread and cut raw meat as the blood and juices from raw meat can contaminate other foods. Plastic chopping boards are the easiest to keep clean and the most hygienic. This applies to different plates, knives and utensils as well.

◆ Allow food to thaw out in the refrigerator in a leak-proof container rather than on the kitchen work surface.

◆ Allow food to thaw thoroughly before cooking.

◆ Always ensure that you follow the manufacturer's cooking instructions, which can be found on the food label, when storing, heating or cooking food.

Remember that boiling point is 100°C and harmful bacteria in food is not destroyed until food has been cooked to a temperature of 71°C. It is absolutely essential that food is cooked thoroughly, at the correct temperature and for the correct length of time to avoid food poisoning.

HAND WASHING

One of the easiest and most effective ways of preventing the spread of infection is by washing hands. However many people do not realize the importance of this simple routine and how, if this is done randomly or rushed, it ceases to be effective.

When to wash hands
Teach your child the importance of washing hands correctly and ensure that they are aware of why it is necessary to wash hands. You should wash your hands:

◆ After blowing noses

◆ After changing a baby's nappy or wiping a child's bottom

◆ After coughing or sneezing

◆ After gardening or playing in sand

◆ After handling babies' feeding bottles

◆ After handling money

◆ After handling or feeding pets

◆ After handling raw or cooked food

◆ After playing outside

◆ After visiting the toilet

◆ Before feeding babies and children

◆ Before you eat

- When dealing with a first aid situation

- When dealing with a minor injury such as a graze

- Whenever hands appear dirty!

Why we wash our hands

Preventing the spread of infection is essential if you are to ensure that your child is healthy and free from illness. Children pick up infections easily and through many means, such as touch, food, water, animals, cuts, grazes and droplets in the air. It has to be said that most children's hygiene methods leave a lot to be desired! Encourage your child to wash their hands often and explain the reasons behind this necessity.

How we wash our hands

When teaching your child to wash their hands follow these simple rules:

- Wet hands thoroughly with hot water before applying soap.

- Use liquid soap if at all possible as this is more hygienic than bars of soap which have a tendency to harbour bacteria if allowed to sit in water for any length of time.

- Massage both hands with lather paying special attention to fingernails, thumbs and between the fingers.

- If rings are worn, these should either be removed and washed separately or washed underneath whilst on the finger.

- Rinse hands well under running water before drying.

- Each person should have their own towel.

It is advisable to wear plastic gloves when dealing with urine, blood, faeces etc. however, hands should still be washed thoroughly even if gloves have been worn.

To wash hands correctly the whole process should take a minimum of 30 seconds. Encourage children to time themselves by leaving an egg timer or stop watch by the sink until they have learned to recognize the acceptable length of time needed for successfully washing hands.

ANIMAL SAFETY

Animals form a large part of many families and, when treated with consideration, they can become much loved members of the family. It is important to remember at all times, however, that they are animals and, as such, they can be unpredictable. Even the friendliest of dogs for example, can react violently if hurt whether this is intentional or not. If you have pets in your home make sure that they are tolerant of children and that you teach your child to respect them. Animals are not toys and you should never allow your child to tease or annoy a pet. Children should be encouraged to care for animals and, when old enough, learn how to clean their cages and feed them.

Animal and child safety guidelines

By following these simple guidelines you will be able to ensure that your children and pets live in harmony with one another:

♦ Never leave young children alone with pets no matter how friendly you consider the animal to be. No one can predict how an animal will react if it is hurt even if this is done unintentionally.

♦ Discourage children from feeding pets from their plate and, whenever possible, make sure that pets are not allowed in the same room whilst you are eating.

♦ Ensure that pets have their own feeding bowls and that these are washed separately from the rest of the family dishes.

- Make sure that children wash their hands after being in contact with pets.

- Ensure that your pets see a vet regularly and that dogs and cats are treated for worms and fleas periodically.

- Ensure that you clean up after your pet immediately. Pets, like humans, can get sick and have 'accidents'. If this is the case, use disinfectant to clean up and dispose of everything immediately and hygienically.

EQUIPMENT SAFETY

The market is absolutely saturated with equipment and devices aimed at parents, and it is probably true to say that new parents, in particular, feel slightly daunted at the prospect of choosing the right kind of equipment and accessories for their child. One of the most important things to remember is that, used correctly following the manufacturers' guidelines, *most* equipment on the market today should be safe. It is essential that any equipment or toys you purchase for your child conform to British safety standards. The easiest way to do this is to make sure that you look for one of the safety symbols such as the 'kite', 'lion' or 'CE' mark on all items before you buy them. Take extra care if you are buying toys and equipment from car boot sales or jumble sales.

Guidelines for toys and equipment

The following guidelines will help you to ensure that the toys and equipment you buy are safe and free from potential dangers.

Toys

Toys are the cause of thousands of accidents a year. Tripping over toys left on floors or allowing young children to play with toys which are inappropriate for their age and stage of development are just some of the ways in which toys can be dangerous. Make sure that clutter on the floor is kept to a minimum and encourage children to put toys away before allowing them to get something else out. Despite the Toys Safety Regulations 1995 it is still possible for unsafe, illegal toys to be purchased in England and you should take special care when selecting toys for young children.

Make sure there are no small parts which can wear or become loose and check the age range on the packaging to ensure their suitability. Never be tempted to purchase a toy which is aimed at an older child even if your child is highly intelligent and may well enjoy such a toy. It may contain small parts which can pose a choking hazard. Remember guidelines are there to be considered, not ignored.

Extra care should be taken with regard to battery operated toys. Always make sure that young children can not gain access to the batteries, particularly the small mercury disc batteries, as these can easily be swallowed. Make sure you dispose of spent batteries carefully – never burn them – and always use the correct batteries for each toy.

Avoid purchasing dolls and soft toys with lots of hair as this can pose a choking hazard for young children.

Buggies
Make sure that buggies and prams are in a good state of repair and that these conform to the British safety standards. Always use reins to securely fasten children in and check regularly for worn or missing parts. If you purchase a 'buggy board' designed to carry a toddler on the back of your buggy make sure that this is correctly fitted and that it is suited to your make of pushchair.

Car seats
Never buy car seats from second-hand shops or car boot sales as you have no way of telling whether they are safe. Ensure that you know how to fit your child's car seat correctly and follow the manufacturer's instructions at all times.

Baby walkers
Many parents swear by baby walkers, however there is no evidence to suggest that they assist a child in walking. Some people believe

that the opposite is true and that baby walkers actually hinder the walking progress. What is certain however is that walkers can be potentially very dangerous. If you do intend to purchase a baby walker make sure that your child only uses it under strict supervision and that the floor is flat – no stairs – and free of clutter. The area where they are used should be clear of furniture and other potential hazards such as fires. I personally would not advise anyone to use a baby walker as the potential for children to over-balance in them and tip them over is very high.

Safety gates

Although safety gates are intended to assist with the safety of the child, care should be taken when selecting which gates to purchase. Safety gates are very important pieces of equipment and it is essential that the gates fit securely and that the fastenings are firm and child proof. It is preferable to choose an opening gate, rather than one you climb over.

Highchair

Another important piece of equipment. Highchairs should be suitable for the size and weight of the child that they are intended for. The child should be securely fastened in using a safety harness, which will need to be adjusted to fit the child comfortably as they grow. Always make sure that highchairs are placed on a flat, even floor and that they do not wobble or tip. Table-mounted chairs should be used with caution as these can be very unstable. Baby seats should always be placed on a flat even floor and never placed on tables or work surfaces. Babies and children should always be securely fastened into a baby seat.

Potties

An important part of toilet training for many children; potties should be free from cracks or splits. Child toilet seats, which are designed to fit over an adult toilet seat, must also be checked for cracks and splits and children should never be allowed to climb in order to reach the toilet. Provide a non-slip step for children to reach the toilet safely

SAFETY CHECKLIST IN THE HOME

Make sure your child is safe by following these rules:

✓ Supervise your child at all times – remember babies and children learn by exploring their surroundings and it is up to you to keep them away from danger.

✓ Eliminate as many potential dangers in your home as possible. Teach your child about potential dangers and how they can keep safe from an early age.

✓ Babies and young children have no understanding of danger!

2

Keeping Your Child Safe in the Garden

As with the home, the garden can be fraught with danger. Young children love to explore and the garden can hold endless adventures and fascination. However, parents need to be vigilant when allowing their children the freedom to play outdoors and, once again, supervision is the key factor to ensuring safety.

KEEPING YOUR GARDEN HAZARD FREE

Unlike parks and public playgrounds, it should be relatively easy to ensure that your own garden is kept hazard free, as you and your family will usually have sole use of this area. In order to make sure that your children are safe in the garden, however, you will need to check it regularly and keep up with mowing the lawn and weeding the flower beds. If you live in an area where litter is a problem, make sure that you pick up any litter which has blown or been dropped into your garden. In particular, look out for empty beer cans and bottles and cigarette butts which passers by may, from time to time, decide to throw over your garden gate or fence.

CREATING A CHILD-FRIENDLY GARDEN

It is possible to create a child-friendly, inviting garden area where children will enjoy endless hours of fun in the fresh air. Children do not need expensive outdoor toys and equipment and are often just as happy digging for worms in a damp patch of soil. Outdoor play is essential for children and the possibilities for learning in the outdoor environment are endless.

CARRYING OUT A RISK ASSESSMENT

It is, however, essential that you carry out a risk assessment of your garden in much the same way as you would your home in order to eliminate not only the obvious dangers but also those which are often overlooked. Your garden needs to be free from poisonous plants, litter, debris, water hazards etc. and this chapter will look at ways of creating and maintaining a child-friendly outdoor play area.

COMMON DANGERS IN THE GARDEN

Ponds

Although ponds can be an interesting garden feature which can hold endless fascination for children of all ages, they are also extremely dangerous. They should be avoided in a family garden unless the whole pond area can be fenced off safely to prevent children from gaining access. Remember that children can drown in only a few centimetres of water and, therefore, the risk is not simply just from deep ponds or rivers. Pond features created in tubs or barrels or small fountains can be equally hazardous to young children.

Dustbins

It goes without saying that children should not be allowed to play in dustbins. However, think carefully about where you position your dustbins. Do they pose a threat from climbing? Can children get inside them? Wheelie bins make great dens when empty, providing a good place to hide, which can result in an accident. If possible, fence off a designated area for your dustbins and make sure that children cannot gain access to them.

Greenhouses

Greenhouses can prove a real headache. If you have a greenhouse make sure that it is sited well away from the area to be used by your children. Greenhouses can cause major problems if children fall against them or break the glass with play equipment. Consider fitting glass safety film to your greenhouse.

Sheds

Sheds are another source of endless fascination for young children. They can be extremely dangerous places and children should never be allowed to play in them unsupervised. Weedkiller, lawnmowers, garden forks, shears, garden twine, slug pellets, strimmers: the list is endless. Every one of these objects could be potentially lethal if in the wrong hands. Make sure that garden insecticides are kept in their original packaging and locked in a cabinet or stored out of the reach of children and always keep your shed locked. You may like to consider erecting a small wendy house for your children to play in to discourage them from playing in the one where gardening equipment is stored. If you do get a wendy house, keep it solely for the children and do not be tempted to use it as an 'overspill' from the main shed.

Drains

Never allow children to play in or near drains. Fit drain covers to all drains which are accessible to children. Apart from the obvious risk of infection, small fingers can become lodged in the grates if children are allow to play in and around drains.

Gates and fences

One of the easiest and most effective ways of keeping children safe in the garden is to prevent them from getting out. A gate with a faulty catch or a broken fence is an opportunity of escape for a young child and the dangers beyond the garden are infinitely more sinister than those within its confines. Mend fences and fit secure catches to gates to ensure that your garden area is secure and that children can not wander out onto the street.

Play equipment

Lots of families install expensive play equipment for their children and, whilst this is all very nice if finances allow, it is paramount that parents think carefully not just of what they intend to buy but how they intend to install it. Swings, slides and climbing frames should be securely fastened to the ground to prevent the equipment from tipping over when in use. A suitable ground covering such as bark chippings or astroturf should be used under all such equipment to cushion a child in the event of a fall. Check outdoor play equipment regularly for wear and tear and replace or repair any missing or worn parts. This is particularly important after the winter months when the equipment may have been standing unused for some time. Rusty, corroded equipment is a danger to children.

Bicycles and other ride-on toys

Make sure that any outdoor toys and equipment you purchase for your child are suitable for their current age. Never be tempted to purchase a bike which is too big for your child to ride with the intention that they will 'grow into it'. Chances are that they will encounter endless accidents learning to ride a bike which is inappropriate and, if they haven't been put off bicycles by the time they are big enough to use it safely, they will certainly have seen their fair share of cuts and bruises. If you are going to the expense of purchasing a bicycle for your child only do so if your finances stretch to a helmet as well. Helmets should be worn at all times when riding bicycles and, if your child is learning to ride for the first time, you may even like to consider purchasing elbow and knee pads for those inevitable falls.

Plants

Avoid planting any plants which may be poisonous if eaten or touched and, if your garden does contain any such plants, remove them immediately. Although not all plants or shrubs with berries are poisonous, it is a good idea to avoid these as they often appear attractive to children who may swallow them. Any plants with prickles or thorns should also be avoided for obvious reasons. The list below gives *some* of the more common plants which should be avoided in a child-friendly garden:

◆ Angel's trumpets

◆ Autumn crocus

- Castor oil plant
- Daffodil bulbs
- Deadly nightshade
- Foxglove
- Glory lily
- Hellebore
- Hemlock
- Hyacinth
- Laburnum
- Lily of the valley
- Monkshood
- Oleander
- Poinsettia
- Poison primrosc
- Rhubarb leaves
- Rue
- Thorn apple
- Winter cherry
- Woody nightshade
- Yew

PROTECTING YOUR CHILD FROM DROWNING

It is a fact that children can drown in just a few centimetres of water and small ornamental ponds, water butts and garden water features can be just as hazardous as swimming pools and lakes. Indeed, it is often these smaller water features which prove to be the most dangerous as these are regularly overlooked and attention to safety here is often lacking. Homes lucky enough to have an outdoor swimming pool will probably have all the safety features installed and the area will either be fenced off or covered to ensure that children cannot fall in and drown. However, what safety measures have you put in place for your water feature in a barrel or your small 3 foot by 2 foot ornamental fishpond? A child can trip, bang their head and fall into a pond this size just as easily as they can fall into an Olympic-sized swimming pool. The chances are that the fish pond will have little or no safety measures compared to the swimming pool.

Preventing drowning

Ideally your garden will be free of any water hazards, particularly if you have young children, however if you do have a pond or other water feature it is essential that children are denied access from this area either by fencing it off or using a sturdy grill across the surface of the water. Never be tempted to use a net which will easily give way to the weight of a child if they fall onto it. Grills should be measured and fitted according to the manufacturer's instructions and tested to ensure that they do not collapse when any weight is put on them. Fencing and grills may appear unsightly but, as the need for them is relatively short lived, it is better to be safe than sorry. Ponds can be an excellent way of introducing nature to a child and pond life can hold an endless fascination for some children, that said, it is paramount that you supervise children at all times whilst they are around water. Teach them how to stay safe near water as soon as they are old enough to understand. Never allow children to play games or fool around near ponds or water features and ensure that they are aware of the potential dangers these may pose.

PLAY AREAS

We have looked at play areas briefly at the beginning of this chapter. Many children enjoy the luxury of having an area of the garden designed specifically for them and these areas can be a source of hours of fun and entertainment.

Climbing apparatus

Climbing apparatus such as swings, slides, climbing frames etc. can result in accidents if not used correctly and in conjunction with safety features. As mentioned earlier, the apparatus should be securely fitted to the ground to prevent tipping and a suitable ground covering should be used to cushion any falls. Teach children how to use the apparatus sensibly and encourage them to play safely and considerately to reduce the risk of any accidents.

Trampolines and bouncy castles

Trampolines and bouncy castles are very popular pieces of equipment and can, once again, provide hours of fun and exercise if used correctly. Always use a safety net around trampolines and ensure constant supervision when children are playing on this kind of equipment. Also make sure that the apparatus is not overloaded. Safety nets around trampolines can become damaged and should be repaired or replaced immediately when this happens. Children can easily become entangled in broken safety nets posing a threat of strangulation and, rest assured, if a child does fall they will do so in the area where the net has worked loose and end up crashing to the ground!

SAFETY CHECKLIST IN THE PLAY AREA

- ◆ Children should be taught never to walk in front of a swing.

- ◆ Children should be taught to use slides correctly and not be allowed to climb up the slide but to use the steps.

- ◆ Children should be discouraged from using apparatus as a climbing frame unless this is the purpose it is actually intended for.

- ◆ Never allow children to overload equipment for example one person should use a single seat swing at any one time.

- ◆ Make sure that your child understands the importance of playing safely outdoors and not to take any unnecessary risks. Although outdoor play should be fun children also need to be aware of the potential dangers and how to avoid them.

BARBEQUES

Barbeques, patio heaters and other outdoor heating devices can be very dangerous to children. Never allow a child near these pieces of equipment and always keep a bucket of water handy when barbequing. When not in use, barbeques should be stored safely out of the reach of young children – ideally in a locked shed.

GARDENING

Many children enjoy helping adults in the garden and the educational aspect of gardening is very good. Children can learn a great deal by being allowed to explore the garden. Children should be encouraged to work in the garden with adult supervision and parents should allow their children to plant seeds, water and care for plants.

How to be safe when gardening

◆ If your child shows a keen interest in gardening then buy a child sized fork, spade, trowel etc. as these will be much easier and safer for them to use. Adult sized tools are often much heavier and more difficult to handle and can cause injury to the child.

◆ Select easy-to-grow seeds and plants which will require little nurturing and never purchase plants which can be poisonous.

◆ Supervise children at all times when they are planting seeds and bulbs and ensure that they wash their hands thoroughly after gardening.

◆ Avoid letting young children dig the soil in flower beds and vegetable patches as these can often be used as a toilet for neighbouring cats! Cat faeces can be very dangerous and the risk of infection from being in contact with animal waste is high.

◆ Make sure that children wear gloves in the garden and that they wash their hands thoroughly after each gardening activity.

SAFETY CHECKLIST IN THE GARDEN
✓ Supervise your child at all times.
✓ Create a safe outdoor area free from hazards.
✓ Make sure your garden is enclosed and that the gate is kept shut at all times.
✓ Never leave children alone near ponds, water butts or water features.
✓ Practice safety in the sun.

SUN CARE

Almost everyone loves the summer months when the days are hot and the sun shines endlessly (not a typical British summer, I know!) however, these long lazy days can hold potential dangers for children and adults alike if certain safety measures are not put in place.

Babies and young children burn and become dehydrated very quickly. They should not be exposed to the strong rays of the sun without adequate protection. Never underestimate the strength of the sun or the potential harm it can cause.

The sun emits different kinds of rays, all of which are harmful to our skin.

UVA – These are the sun's rays which cause wrinkles and aging to the skin. UVA rays contribute to cancer such as Melanoma.

UVB – These are the sun's rays which cause sunburn, cataracts and damage to our immune system.

UVC – These are the most dangerous of the sun's rays. However, fortunately the ozone layer blocks them, preventing them from reaching the earth.

◆ **FACT** ◆

Most children rack up between 50 and 80% of their lifetime sun exposure before they reach eighteen years of age. It is therefore extremely important that we teach them how to enjoy fun in the sun safely.

Sunburn

If your child is unfortunate enough to suffer from sunburn they will probably be in some considerable pain and discomfort. By following a few simple steps you should be able to make them more comfortable and address the damage caused:

◆ Keep your child out of the sun until their sunburn has healed *completely*. Exposing already burnt skin to the sun's rays will result in more pain and skin damage.

◆ Bathe your child in cool – not cold – water, or add cool compresses to the sunburnt areas.

◆ Apply aloe vera gel available from chemists to soothe the burnt areas.

◆ Moisturize the skin to rehydrate.

If your child's sunburn is severe and they are experiencing any of the following symptoms, call a doctor immediately:

◆ Blistering

◆ Nausea

◆ Vomiting

◆ Fainting

◆ Delirium

◆ Diarrhoea.

Remember that, even on a dull day when the sun is hidden behind cloud, harmful UV rays still pose a threat as they can travel through the clouds and reflect off sand, water and even concrete. Many people are often tricked into a false sense of security on dull days, however it is essential that you follow the same sun safety rules regardless of whether or not there are clouds in the sky.

SAFETY CHECKLIST IN THE SUN

Keep your child safe in the sun by following these simple rules:

✓ Use sunscreen whenever the sun in shining – choose a minimum of factor 25 for children.

✓ Re-apply sunscreen every 3 to 4 hours and after swimming or playing in water.

✓ Avoid going outside during the hottest part of the day – between 11am and 3pm.

✓ Keep children and babies covered up in strong sunshine.

✓ Provide eye protection.

✓ Make sure that children do not become dehydrated by offering lots of fluids.

✓ Make sure that babies and children always wear a hat.

3

Keeping Your Child Safe Outside the Home

PROTECTING YOUR CHILD OUTSIDE THE HOME

Although much can be done to protect our children in the home and garden many parents worry about their children when they are away from the home setting. When our children are out and about we obviously have much less control over the dangers they face. With regularly reported cases of child abduction, street crime, rape and road accidents, parental concerns are unsurprising. It is, however, impossible for parents to protect their children every minute of every day and there will be times, as our children grow older, when we have to give them some degree of freedom and responsibility.

The important thing to remember is that you need to *prepare* your child and equip them with the necessary knowledge to:

- ◆ avoid dangerous situations

- ◆ know how to handle themselves in dangerous situations

- ◆ know how to report a dangerous situation.

The tricky part is to encourage your child to understand that the world can be a dangerous, violent and unpredictable place without actually frightening them. We cannot wrap our children in cotton wool and protect them from the many dangers they will invariably come across from time to time throughout their lives. What we can do however, is to encourage them to grow up as confident, knowledgeable and sensible young people.

STRANGER DANGER

One of the most frightening aspects faced by parents today is the knowledge that their child may be at risk of harm from a stranger. Although statistics show that children are much more likely to be harmed by someone they know rather than by a complete stranger, newspaper headlines of child abduction and murder are both frightening and abhorrent and the very nature of these crimes, though relatively far and few between, make them stick in our minds and serve as a deep-rooted fear for all parents.

Young children are trusting. They see adults as people who are there to help and protect them and, in an ideal world, a child's vision of adults would indeed be the right one. However, in today's society, children need to be aware of the dangers posed by strangers no matter how insignificant these may be.

Letting your child go out without an adult

It has been reported that children have gone missing from their beds or from their mother's side whilst out shopping, prompting parents to ask how can they be certain their children are safe when they are away from their home and their parents? This is obviously not an easy question to answer and it is one which will depend very much on the age and stage of development each child is at. There is no magical formula for ensuring that children are safe away from the home. What parents can do is to make sure that first and foremost, before allowing their child the freedom to be out and about alone without adult supervision, they are sensible and mature enough to know how to handle themselves and that they are aware of the procedure to follow should they experience any dangers or difficulties. Never allow your child to pressurise you into allowing them out with friends if you are unsure of how they will cope. Try to build up the time they are allowed out and, once they have proven themselves to be sensible, you can increase this time.

Carrying a mobile phone

Often parents will equip their child with a mobile telephone or request that they stay within a certain radius of home so that they can 'report back' at designated intervals. In essence, this is fine as it enables the child to have the freedom they crave whilst alleviating the parent's worry.

However, what we also need to be aware of is that, despite mobile telephones or being made to report back to parents on the hour, the potential dangers of being lured by a stranger are very real. It is essential that we teach our children how to deal with such a situation rather than lead them to believe that simply carrying a mobile telephone is all that is needed to ensure their safety as, of course, sometimes it is these very pieces of equipment which lead to crime in the first instance. By providing your child with a mobile telephone, it may be argued that you are putting them at risk of being mugged for it. However, the advantages of carrying a mobile telephone far outnumber the disadvantages and, provided you teach your child to keep their telephone out of sight and discourage them from walking down the street with it permanently stuck to their ear, then they should avoid this kind of unwanted attention. Children need to be taught that, used correctly, a mobile telephone is an important piece of safety equipment and not simply a fashion accessory.

Reducing the risk of stranger danger

Although it is vital that children know how to respond if they are approached by a stranger it is also very important that they are taught how to reduce the risk to themselves by learning a few preventative measures:

◆ Always make sure that your child tells you where they are going, whom they are going with and when they are likely to return.

◆ Always reiterate the importance of steering clear of lonely places such as woodland, quiet lanes etc.

- When walking down a street, make sure that your child knows to walk on the side of the pavement as far away from the kerb as possible – this will prevent anyone from trying to pull them into a passing car.

- Teach your child not to speak to strangers – both men and women have been known to abduct children therefore children should not speak to either, however kind or polite they appear to be.

- Teach your child never to take sweets or gifts from strangers.

- Inform your child of some of the ploys which strangers may use to entice them away, such as 'I've lost my dog/keys, will you help me find it/them'. Children can be very innocent and trusting and this kind of tactic will often tempt them into helping. Child abductors are very astute and know the best ways of gaining a child's interest and, ultimately, their trust.

- Although fun fairs, amusement arcades, parks and swimming baths are all fun places for children to visit, they are also the kind of places that paedophiles hang around in and extra care should be taken if you are allowing your child to visit these types of settings. If possible make sure that your child is part of a group and that, preferably, an adult will be in attendance.

It is always better that children are prepared for every eventuality, although, hopefully, being approached by a stranger will probably never happen to your child, it is essential that they are aware of how to react should the need arise. You need to stress how important this kind of situation is and you should never 'play down' the seriousness of child abduction nor should you look to use 'scare tactics' on your child. Terrifying a child into never going out is not the way to avoid danger.

What your child should do if they feel threatened

- Make sure that your child knows that it is alright to make a fuss if they feel scared or threatened. Teach them to scream and shout and attract as much attention as possible. This will usually result in their attacker fleeing to avoid recognition and reprimand.

◆ If your child has been grabbed, teach them to struggle, kick, bite, hit and lash out. Not only will this attract attention, which the abductor will want to avoid, but also it may loosen any hold a stranger may have on your child giving them vital seconds to escape.

◆ If your child has something taken from them, such as money or a mobile telephone, teach them to let their possessions go without a fight. No-one can be sure nowadays that a mugger is not carrying a weapon and a lost mobile telephone is nothing in comparison to a lost life. Possessions can be replaced – it is not worth risking serious injury or even death to protect personal possessions.

◆ Make sure that your child knows they are not to blame for the offence. Children can often feel that it is their fault if they find themselves in difficult circumstances and this can be very worrying and stressful to the child in addition to the trauma they have already suffered.

◆ If your child is in distress and needs help, teach them to look for a police officer, traffic warden or any other uniformed personnel. If none are in sight tell them to go into a *busy* shop and to raise the alarm. Under no circumstances should your child knock on the door of a house or flag down a passing car to ask for help.

◆ Teach your child how to call for help using the emergency services – dial 999.

ABDUCTION

It is every parent's worst nightmare that someone may take their child away from them. The death of a child, though unbearable and extremely distressing, is final; whereas the abduction of a child leaves so many questions unanswered and always a glimmer of hope. Parents will often find it impossible to carry on with everyday life despite the passing of days, weeks, months or even years and find themselves clinging onto the slightest chance that they may be reunited with their child.

The recent case in 2007 of a child being taken from a holiday apartment in Portugal highlighted, once again, how easy it is for a child to go missing and how terribly vulnerable they are.

Keeping things in perspective

A survey was carried out in 2007 by the Children's Society – as part of the Good Childhood Inquiry. Many of the parents who took part in the survey were 'free-rein youngsters' themselves during their own childhood, who regularly enjoyed the freedom today's children are denied; however, the survey concluded that parents nowadays consider the acceptable age for children to be allowed out with friends to be 14.

In a relatively short space of time parents have decided that the world is an unsafe place and that their children need much more protection today than they did in their own childhood days. What exactly is the reason for this shift in opinion? Were there less perverts and child molesters prowling around looking for young children thirty years ago or has the world just gone crazy with parents now being over protective towards their children in a way which may be detrimental to their upbringing?

No-one knows for sure, however, one thing we can be certain of is that the world *is* a dangerous place of that there is no doubt. We must also get things into perspective. Not every eight-year-old child who is allowed to go for a picnic with their friends will be the subject of an abduction or encounter a paedophile However, the *possibility* is there and young children need to be made aware of the dangers, how to avoid them and, if necessary, what to do if they run into difficulties. Preparing your child is vital, frightening them is unnecessary and must be avoided lest our children grow up feeling intimidated every time a stranger speaks to them and being fearful of leaving the safety of their homes.

SAFETY CHECKLIST OUTSIDE THE HOME

✓ Always make sure you know where your child is going, whom they are going with and when they will be back.

✓ If possible, equip your child with a mobile telephone.

✓ Teach your child how to attract attention or report incidents which make them feel threatened.

PROTECTION FOR TEENAGE CHILDREN

Going out

The parents who took part in the survey I mentioned earlier in this chapter feel that 14 is an acceptable age for children to be allowed out with friends. However, does this mean that a 13-year-old is particularly vulnerable and a 15-year-old will never face danger? Of course not. It is to be hoped that the average 14-year-old can reasonably be expected to weigh up potential dangers and know how to protect themselves when faced with most situations. The dangers do not go away as the children head into their teens and, in some cases, they actually intensify. Teenage children today are faced with problems such as alcohol, drugs and street crime.

Being prepared

Teenagers may be out alone late at night and they will most certainly need to have their wits about them. Being prepared is the key to safety. Whilst supervision was paramount when your child was little, preparing them for all eventualities is paramount when they are growing up. Talk to your child, make sure they are aware of the many scenarios they may be faced with and that they know how to handle themselves. Encourage them to be sensible and to take control of their lives. Most teenagers enjoy a night out and alcohol is often part of many teenagers' night life. However, it is important that teenagers understand how alcohol can affect the way they think and act and that it is important that they ensure that they do not consume so much alcohol when they are out that they do not have any control over themselves or their actions.

Trusting your teenager

Teenagers need to feel that they are trusted by the adults around them. They need responsibility and acceptance as they are finding their way in an adult world. Try to allow them the freedom they deserve whilst making sure that they are aware that you will worry about them simply because it is your *job* to worry about them. Responsible parents will never stop worrying about their children and it is important that their offspring realize that this is the very nature of being a loving, caring parent. If your child realizes that you have only their best interests at heart and that your are not trying to spoil their fun chances are they will cooperate and may even, deep down, be ever so pleased that they have loving parents who are concerned for their welfare!

Treating your teenager like an adult

If you approach the topic of safety in an adult fashion you are much more likely to get your child's attention and cooperation than if you speak down to them in a fashion that spells out to them that they are the child and you are the adult. Try to think back to how you responded to your own parents as a teenager. If you were cooperative was this because you were treated as an individual and an equal? If your teenager asks permission to go to a party, think carefully before saying 'no'. By denying them the chance to grow up and enjoy normal activities for their age, you risk alienating them and making them sly and resentful. Surely it is better that they ask your permission and allow you to set some rules than to lie about their whereabouts and go behind your back?

If you are going to set down ground rules for your teenager's night out, make sure that these rules are fair. Whenever possible, arrange to collect your child from the party at a set time. *Never* allow young children to travel home alone late at night.

Setting down ground rules for living at home
Deciding when your child is old enough and mature enough for added responsibility is not easy. Young people love to be in charge of their lives and often feel they are 'grown up' long before you recognize them to be. It is not always easy to get your teenager to agree to tell you where they are going and they may not always understand the importance of abiding by certain rules. However, it is important that you explain to your child why it is necessary to have these rules and that they understand that they are in place for their own protection.

You need to show your child that you trust them. However, trust needs to be earned and built upon, and it is important that you talk to your child in order to build a good relationship with them. Avoid being didactic, but make it clear that your rules are there for a reason and by telling you where they are going and, when they are likely to be home, they will be eliminating the need for you to worry or put a ban on them going out. Ground rules are important for everyone.

Anti-social behaviour

However much you love your child there will be times, particularly during their teenage years, when you may not like their behaviour or you may simply feel that you do not really know who they are. Your once loving, open and affectionate child can literally turn into a rude, truanting teenager dabbling with alcohol and drugs and exhibiting completely unacceptable anti-social behaviour. There are many causes for bad behaviour in teenagers and sometimes every day may feel like an upward struggle both for you and for them.

Factors which contribute to anti-social behaviour included:

◆ An unstable family life
◆ Divorce
◆ Peer pressure
◆ Boredom
◆ Problems at school
◆ Bullying.

Preventing anti-social behavoiur

Although it is relatively easy to list the factors which may cause your teenager to suddenly go 'off the rails', it is important to remember that preventing such behaviour is often much easier than finding a cure for it. It is vital that you keep an open relationship with your teenager and, even when they are unwilling to talk, make sure that they know that you are there for them and that you can and will help them if necessary. You must learn to work with your child, however much you may dislike their behaviour. Avoid being judgemental but explain how their behaviour is affecting not just themselves but every member of the family and that you want to help them to get their lives back on track. This may not be easy and it can take many months, sometimes even years, but without your help they may never achieve their full potential.

For their own safety it is better to stop your child from ever getting involved in crime or mixing with the wrong people who may have an adverse affect on their behaviour. A good, stable home life with loving parents who take an active interest in their child is one of the best ways of steering young children and teenagers out of danger and in to a positive way of life.

Discovering sexuality

Another potentially worrying phase that some teenagers may go through is when they experience a range of emotions and may discover that they are gay or bisexual. Parents faced with this prospect may feel shocked, worried, ashamed, embarrassed and they may even find it difficult to accept the truth. From a safety point of view you may be concerned about HIV/AIDS and bullying.

'Coming out' is a big step for any young person and your child may have been battling their feelings for years before finally giving in and accepting their own identity. Your child will need your support. Your child's sexual preferences are not an illness and are not a result of the way you have brought them up. Guilt should not be an issue here. Forcing your child to hide their feelings or taking the attitude that they are simply 'going through a phase' and 'will grow out of it soon' will only result in damaging their self-confidence in the long term. As a parent you need to accept your child's sexuality, listen to what they have to say and offer all the support they need.

Depression and mental health

The teenage years are difficult ones fraught with physical, mental and emotional issues. Whilst most teenagers appear to cope well with the highs and lows that life throws at them, a small proportion find everyday issues more difficult to cope with and the result for them is depression.

Teenagers and young adults do not have the experience to deal with many of the everyday issues they are faced with and they can be sensitive and vulnerable.

Signs of depression

There are many signs of depression which parents should be aware of such as:

- ◆ becoming morbid and seemingly obsessed with death
- ◆ experiencing difficulty sleeping
- ◆ experiencing mood swings
- ◆ increase in appetite (comfort eating)
- ◆ loss of appetite
- ◆ reluctance to socialize
- ◆ seeming unhappy
- ◆ showing little interest in the things around them
- ◆ struggling with school work
- ◆ unduly quiet and withdrawn.

Sometimes teenagers who are depressed seek a way out of their misery by seeking solace in alcohol or drugs or they may become abusive and violent and resort to crime.

Supporting your depressed child

You will need to show immense patience and understanding if your child is suffering from depression. Make sure that they know that you are there for them and that you are prepared to listen should they wish to talk. More importantly, make sure that they know that their worries will be taken seriously and that you will help and support them in any way necessary. Many children can become depressed and worry about things such as exams, friendships, problems at home, feeling unloved etc. It is important to remember that what may seem inconsequential to us may be very important to your child.

Depression is an illness and if your child is suffering from depression they need help. Don't try to ignore the problem hoping it will get better or go away as this may result in the depression deepening and becoming out of control. Your child may even end up contemplating suicide. If your child cannot talk to you, make sure that they are aware of the helplines available and encourage them to see their doctor or school nurse.

Eating disorders

Eating disorders can be an issue for anyone regardless of their sex or age. However, young people are very vulnerable to developing eating disorders as they often see food as a way of dealing with other personal problems they may be experiencing. Controlling their food intake is sometimes the only part of their lives they feel they can be in charge of.

Eating disorders fall into two main categories:

> **Anorexia** This is when a person weighs at least 15% less than they should. It is a very serious condition which, if not dealt with, can lead to life-long health problems and even death.

> **Bulimia** This is when a person binge eats in secret. Their body weight usually remains the same as the sufferer purposely makes themselves sick after bingeing on food. Once again, if not treated, bulimia can lead to life-long health problems.

Signs of anorexia
Warning signs of anorexia include:

◆ Avoiding mealtimes
◆ Dental problems
◆ Difficulty sleeping
◆ Excessive weight loss
◆ Loss of periods in girls
◆ Mood swings
◆ Obsessing (thinking about one issue in particular all the time)
◆ Pretending to have eaten already
◆ Thinning hair.

Signs of bulimia
Warning signs of bulimia include:

◆ Binge eating
◆ Dental problems
◆ Disappearing after meals (to make themselves sick)
◆ Loss of periods in girls
◆ Puffy skin
◆ Sore throat/infections of the throat
◆ Use of laxatives.

Eating disorders can affect both males and females although the problem is more common amongst females. There may be many triggers for eating disorders such as:

◆ Family problems

◆ Abuse

◆ Bullying

◆ Lack of self-esteem

◆ Peer pressure

◆ Wanting to look like a favoured celebrity

- Striving to be popular. (Often teenagers believe that if they are slim and attractive they will make more friends.)

- Exceptionally high expectations from parents. A high percentage of people who suffer from anorexia are high achievers and parents should avoid pushing their child too hard at school/college.

Leaving home

Many teenagers living at home today take it for granted that they will have a bed to sleep in, food to eat and clean clothes to wear. Most will have little or no understanding of the cost of things and will probably have no idea how much you spend on heating, water, telephone calls etc. When the time comes for them to leave home then it is no surprise that many teenagers are in for a shock. Whether your child leaves home to go to college/university, to get married or co-habit or is simply ready to move out of the family home, there is no doubt that, as a parent, you will worry about their safety.

First and foremost you need to help your child to understand that, although they are entering into a new and exciting stage of their lives, they are also taking on an enormous amount of responsibility. By preparing your child, in advance, for the inevitable day when they 'fly the nest' you will be doing them a great service. Your child will need to know how to manage their money and budget for their rent, food, clothes, nights out etc. They will need to know how to look after themselves, how to cook and eat healthy food and how to enjoy their freedom sensibly and safely.

Talk to your child and prepare them for when they leave home. Remind them how lonely living away from home can be and that they are welcome to return home for visits whenever they feel the need. Encourage them to telephone often and to build up a good support network of friends and family who they can call on for help and advice.

Missing from home

There may be times when your child goes missing from home. This may be a case of a simple misunderstanding when they have 'forgotten' to tell you that they were going out and, after the initial frantic search, you track them down at their friends, reprimand them and breathe a sigh of relief. However there are cases when a child deliberately runs away from home and this is often seen as a cry for help. Children can run away from home for any number of reasons including:

◆ Following an argument with a parent or sibling

◆ To escape from violence at home

◆ Experiencing abuse

◆ Experiencing bullying.

If your child starts to stay out late or goes missing for a night or two before returning home with no explanation of their whereabouts, you should be very concerned as these are classic signs that your child may be in trouble. In an ideal world all parents would know where their children are at all times of the day and night; they would know who their friends are and when they are likely to return home. Sadly, this is not always the case.

Children who frequently go missing from home are at danger from:

◆ Drug abuse

◆ Alcohol abuse

◆ Sexual abuse

◆ Sexual exploitation – drawn into prostitution

◆ Crime.

They may be sleeping rough and having to resort to stealing or begging for food.

Teenage pregnancy

The United Kingdom has the highest teenage pregnancy rate in Europe. It comes of no surprise therefore that many parents worry about their teenage children and how they can prevent them from experimenting too early.

Talking to your child about sex

The more information your child has, the less likely they are to have sex too early. Whilst the easiest way to inform your child is to talk to them, not all families find it easy to talk about sexual issues together. If you find it difficult to talk to your child about sex and contraception then try using magazine articles and television programmes to introduce certain topics. Remember also that most children now learn about sex and relationships at school. If your child asks you a question relating to sex and relationships it is important to forget about your own feelings and embarrassment and to answer them honestly. Knowledge is the key and it is important that you teach your child that sex should not be something which is entered into because of peer pressure but that it should be part of a loving, committed relationship.

Other risks of unprotected sex

In addition to unwanted pregnancies, your child is at risk in other ways by having unprotected sex early.

They may become infected with a sexually transmitted disease or may be emotionally affected – children who enter into a sexual relationship early are not emotionally mature to deal with their feelings.

DANGERS ON THE ROAD

In 2001, more than 3,000 children under the age of 16 were seriously injured as pedestrians on the road. It is absolutely vital that you teach your child road safety from a very early age. Road accidents are the biggest single cause of accidental death amongst children and make up for almost half of all fatalities.

Walking and cycling are both great ways of improving your child's health and fitness, however children must learn how to cycle safely and how to use the roads sensibly.

Talk to your child about the dangers on the road and explain to them that, even when crossing on a pedestrian crossing, they must still have their wits about them and remain vigilant as not all drivers are good drivers and accidents can happen anywhere on the road.

SAFETY CHECKLIST ON THE ROAD

Teach your child to:

✓ Use pedestrian crossings whenever possible

✓ Follow the Green Cross Code

✓ Never cross between parked cars, blind spots or bends

✓ Never mess around with friends on a busy road

✓ Wear a helmet at all times when cycling.

4

BULLYING

Bullying is a type of aggressive behaviour which causes profound distress to the victim. Bullying is very serious and should never be ignored. Attacks do not have to be physical in order to cause lasting harm and to seriously undermine a child's confidence or self-esteem. Often verbal abuse, taunting and intimidation can be just as hurtful and distressing as an actual physical attack.

The most common place for your child to suffer at the hands of bullies is at school. Many children suffer bullying at school from time to time and 'fall outs' amongst friends are not uncommon in any age group. However it is when these misunderstandings are blown out of proportion or when a child is picked on for no apparent reason that bullying can become very serious.

BEING ATTENTIVE TO CHANGES IN BEHAVIOUR

As a parent you need to be attentive to the changes in your child and look out for any signs of bullying. Not every disagreement with a friend will result in bullying. Children 'make up' as often as they fall out and this is, of course, all part of growing up, finding ourselves and being allowed to make choices and have opinions.

If you are the kind of parent who has a good relationship with their child and your child feels they can open up to you and tell you things that are worrying them then you are in a very fortunate position. It is highly likely that you will be aware of any bullying immediately and you should be able to sort things out before they escalate. However, it is important to remember that some children try to hide the fact that they are suffering at the hands of bullies.

They think that by complaining or drawing attention to the problem it will make things worse and they will suffer repercussions. No child should be made to suffer in this way and the feelings and torment that victims go through as a result of bullying can be long lasting and extremely damaging.

REASSURING YOUR CHILD

Children who are being bullied need reassurance. They need to know that the adults they confide in will take them seriously and help them to resolve the situation. If your child tells you they are being bullied it is inappropriate and completely unhelpful to tell them to 'fight back' or 'stand up for themselves'. If you are the kind of parent who would be likely to respond in this way the chances are your child will not seek your help and will continue to suffer at the hands of the bully until things get completely out of hand.

WHAT CONSTITUTES BULLYING?

As I have previously mentioned, bullying does not necessarily have to be in the form of a physical attack. Bullying can also be social, psychological or verbal and can take the form of:

◆ Damage to property

◆ Intimidation

◆ Name calling

◆ Racial insults

◆ Sarcasm

◆ Spreading rumours

◆ Teasing

◆ Theft of possessions

◆ Threatening behaviour.

The above forms of bullying are in addition to the physical attacks which may be suffered such as punching, hitting, kicking and hair pulling. Bullying can also be carried out in the form of threats or taunts sent in messages by mobile telephones.

WHAT DOES IT FEEL LIKE TO BE BULLIED?

First and foremost bullying *hurts*. Whether the child is being physically harmed or experiencing name calling and taunts, the actual feeling of being bullied is very hurtful. The victim will feel:

◆ Helpless

◆ Scared

◆ Upset

◆ Worried

◆ Worthless.

They may also feel as if no-one takes them seriously and that they have no-one to turn to or talk to. It is at times likes these that some children feel so alone and so utterly despairing that they start to self-mutilate and may even attempt to take their own lives.

WHO IS AFFECTED BY BULLYING?

Bullying can affect any child at any time, though it is more likely for a child to be bullied in school. Children may be bullied because they appear 'different' from their peers. They may have coloured skin, practise a certain religion or have a disability. However not all bullied children have obvious differences and a substantial number of cases where a child reports bullying states that the tormentor is a former friend. A bully does not have to be older than the child and, in many cases, the bully is usually of a similar age to their victim.

Everyone is affected

Bullying does not just affect the victim or those directly involved, it affects *everyone.* The victim, the bully, the parents of both, their families, teachers and even other children who have witnessed bullying are affected by this type of unacceptable behaviour. For a young person to witness someone being bullied can be very traumatic. They are placed in an extremely compromising situation which could affect them deeply: if they intervene then they run the risk of having the tables turned on them by becoming the victim; if they ignore the behaviour or stand around and watch then they may feel helpless and even guilty for condoning it.

Teach your child not to accept bullying. Advise them to walk away and tell an adult what is happening to them. Tell them not to get into a fight.

THE VICTIM

Unless a child openly tells you that they are being bullied it can sometimes be very difficult to recognize when a child is suffering in this way, particularly if the bullying is not physical and there are no actual visible scars. However the emotional and psychological suffering can be just as hurtful and damaging as any visible wounds.

Being accepted

School days are a time when children need to be accepted by their peers. What other children say and do is very important to them as is being accepted as one of 'the crowd'. Sadly we seem to live in a society where people are picked on and bullied if they are thought of as being 'different'. This can mean anything from the stigma of a disability to the colour of someone's skin or even whether or not they wear glasses. As a parent you should be very careful not to pass on your own racist or prejudiced thoughts. Often this is done unintentionally, but it gives out the wrong messages and highlights the differences in people which, all too often, become the cause for name calling and teasing etc.

How the victim of bullying behaves

Children who are being bullied may act in very different ways. Some children cope admirably in the face of adversity and may be able to shrug off name calling, taunts and hair pulling whilst others will take this kind of treatment very much to heart and become withdrawn and uncooperative. Tragically, a child who feels they have nowhere to turn and no-one to confide in may feel that self-harm or even suicide is the only answer to their suffering and this is, of course, what we should be trying to avoid at all costs. The press and television report about children committing suicide as a result of suffering from bullies on a regular basis. Although schools, out-of-school settings, clubs etc. should all have anti-bullying policies and procedures to follow, these are not always a deterrent. In addition, if the victim chooses to keep quiet about their suffering, then there appears to be very little which can be done.

TIP

Talk to your child every day after school. Discuss the day's events and encourage them to tell you what they have been up to. This will make it easier for you to determine whether anything is wrong and whether they are suffering from any form of bullying or indeed if they are resorting to bullying others themselves.

HOW YOU CAN HELP YOUR CHILD IF THEY ARE BEING BULLIED

If your child tells you that they are being bullied or you have reason to believe that they are, then you must work together to find a suitable strategy for dealing with the situation. Some children will insist that you 'do not make a fuss' for fear of repercussions and may not allow you to speak to their teachers. Whenever possible, try not to go against their wishes but if you feel it is necessary to talk to your child's teachers never lie to your child about your intentions or tell them that you won't speak to the school when you have every intention of doing so. This will result in them feeling betrayed yet again only this time by someone they love and trust and whom they are relying on for help.

Talk to your child and ask them what they would like you to do. Explain that you feel it may be better to speak directly to the school in order that they can keep an eye on things. They could also deal with any bullying issues within the school in accordance with the policies and procedures they have in place. However, if your child becomes distraught at this suggestion and is absolutely adamant that notifying the school is not what they want, then work out a plan together to deal with the situation.

STRATEGIES FOR COPING WITH BULLYING

All parents would be advised to contact the school regardless of their child's preference. If the child is suffering severely at the hands of bullies and is being physically attacked, it is highly likely that this behaviour has been witnessed on school premises. Procedures should already be in place to combat the problem. Depending on the severity of the bullying you may like to adopt some of the following strategies with your child:

Supporting your child
Reassure your child that you love them and that you are on their side 100%. Reassure your child that they are not to blame for the bullying they are experiencing.

Offer lots of praise and encouragement. A child who is being bullied will be stripped of their self-esteem and may feel useless and even deserving of the suffering they are receiving.

Discussing the bullying context
Discuss the build up to the bullying situations. Find out if there are any 'triggers' which appear to be starting the attacks. Sometimes a

child can unintentionally goad or aggravate their attacker and it is necessary to establish whether your child is unwittingly making themselves a target for the bully.

Work out with your child ways of minimising opportunities for the bullying to take place. Encourage your child to spend as much time as possible around other people and tell them to avoid being alone in places where the bully is likely to 'hang out'.

Forging friendships

Is your child quiet and reserved? Do they lack friends or close companions and spend a lot of their time alone? If this is the case then try inviting some of their classmates to your house for tea so that they can get to know your child outside of school. Hopefully friendships can be forged in this way. It is important however to respect your child's need for privacy and never force friendships onto them if they are not happy.

Encouraging assertiveness

Encourage your child to be more assertive. This should not be mistaken for being aggressive. Children do not need to fight to be assertive. They simply need to recognise that they do not have to put up with being mistreated and that they have the right to be treated with respect. There is more about assertiveness on page 70.

Controlling reactions

Try to discourage your child from crying in front of the bully or responding to their threats and behaviour as this can quite often encourage them. Bullies enjoy seeing their victims become distressed and upset and this is the kind of response they are looking for. Insist that your child walks away and, if possible, get them to tell an adult immediately.

Being prepared

Encourage your child to be prepared for the bully's taunts. Quite often a child who has a planned response will feel more in control of the situation and begin to feel more assertive. Being prepared may also catch the bully off guard and dissuade them from carrying out their usual taunts.

Confiding in an adult

Encourage your child to confide in a favourite teacher, someone they can talk to and feel confident about, if they are unsure of taking their problems directly to the head teacher.

Diverting attention

Use diversion tactics when your child is away from school so that they do not spend their time worrying or dwelling on the issues. Encourage them to join clubs to make friends outside of school and help to build their confidence.

SPOTTING THE SIGNS OF BULLYING

If you are a 'hands on' parent who takes an active interest in your child's well being then it is probably true to say that you will notice any significant changes in their behaviour. All children will go through some change in their lifetime as this is all part of growing up. Children will go through phases of being pleasant and helpful to being cheeky, non-committal and downright lazy depending on their age. However, these 'normal' childhood changes should not be viewed with mass hysteria by parents who wrongly assume that their child is being bullied. Parents need to get things into perspective and exercise some control over their assumptions in order to determine whether or not their child really is being subjected to bullying. If you have an open and honest relationship with your child and, when you ask them if they are being bullied they say 'no', then take their word for it. Don't push them into saying something that isn't true, count your blessings and give them time – they will open up to you eventually if something is bothering them.

Indirect signs of bullying

Although some children will tell their parents directly that they are being bullied, others will try to let you know is a more roundabout way such as by saying that they don't want to go to school or they no longer want to go to a certain club.

Other possible signs of bullying include:

- ◆ Unexplained injuries – these could be a sign of physical harm either by a bully or self-inflicted. You should be concerned if your child suddenly appears to be suffering from a lot of injuries for which they can not offer a satisfactory explanation.

- ◆ Ripped clothing.

- ◆ Frequently 'losing' possessions – this could be a sign of having had their possessions stolen by the bully.

- ◆ Often appearing hungry – this could be a sign of having their lunch or lunch money stolen from them by the bully.

- ◆ Complaints of illness such as tummyache and headache – children often feign illness to avoid having to go to school if they are being bullied.

- ◆ Being physically sick – this could be as a result of worry or may be self-inflicted to avoid having to go to school.

- ◆ Showing aggressive behaviour which is otherwise out of character for the child.

- ◆ Suffering from troubled sleep or nightmares.

- ◆ Bedwetting.

- ◆ Becoming withdrawn.

- ◆ Regularly asking for or stealing money – this may be requested from them by the bully often to avoid recrimination.

- ◆ Attempting to self-harm.

- ◆ Deterioration of school work – if your child is usually hard working and does well in class but suddenly starts to lose interest and their school work is suffering you should be concerned.

- ◆ Regression – thumb sucking, rocking, comfort behaviour etc. is often a sign of uncertainty in a child who does not usually resort to this type of behaviour.

Using your judgement

Although the above gives some idea of the signs you should be concerned with, it is by no means an exhaustive list and you will need to use your own parenting skills to ascertain whether your child is acting out of character. If you are concerned about your child's behaviour always talk to them first and try to find out what is bothering them. Often children who are determined to keep things to themselves will open up when confronted by a loving parent who is clearly concerned for their welfare.

Prioritizing your child's feelings

As a parent you may feel angry, upset, helpless or responsible for what your child is going through. You will probably be shocked and hurt that they have not confided in you at the outset. You may even feel that it is your fault for not having spotted the signs earlier and been there to help your child. Although these feelings are common and understandable it is important that you are not overly concerned with how *you* are feeling but that you deal with the problem immediately and seek the help and support necessary for your child.

What is very important, if you suspect that your child is being bullied, is that you must *never* ignore the problem, hoping that it will go away. You must take action and work with your child to find the best solution. You may be of the opinion that your child will never be bullied however, the reality is that bullying can happen to *any* child at *any* time.

HELPING YOUR CHILD IF THEY ARE EXPERIENCING BULLYING:

◆ Always take your child seriously and listen to what they have to say.

◆ Avoid promising to keep the bullying a secret.

◆ Reassure your child that you will help them to sort out the problem.

◆ Practise assertiveness techniques with your child. (See page 70 for information on this.)

◆ Encourage your child to minimize opportunities for bullying to take place, for example, discourage them from taking valuable possessions to school, avoid being alone in the changing rooms and corridors and stay with a group whenever possible.

◆ Give your child responsibility to encourage them to feel valued.

◆ Offer lots of love and praise.

◆ Show compassion and patience.

THE BULLY

Some people would argue that the bully too needs help and that they themselves are probably suffering in some way which results in them taking out their insecurities and frustrations on another child. However, this kind of remark is far from helpful if you are the parent of a child who is being mercilessly persecuted by a bully. The bully's own problems and inadequacies will probably be the very last thing on your mind. However, how would you feel if you discovered that someone else's child is being bullied and that the person doing the bullying is *your* child? Your feelings may well be very similar to those you would feel if your child was the victim only this time the tables have been turned. It is important therefore, in order for parents to help both bullies and their victims, to understand what makes a child resort to bullying and how we can help to put a stop to it.

One of the fundamental things which all parents should remember is that both a child who is being bullied and a child who resorts to bullying both need lots of:

- ◆ Encouragement
- ◆ Love
- ◆ Patience
- ◆ Praise
- ◆ Support.

If the percentage of children being bullied in our schools is high then it goes without saying that the percentage of children doing the bullying must also be unacceptable.

WHY CHILDREN BECOME BULLIES

Children can become bullies for lots of different reasons. They may have family problems, they may be insecure and feel bad about themselves, they may lack confidence and self-esteem, they may even be bullied themselves. Although there is no excuse for such behaviour, it is necessary for us to understand what makes a child become a bully and how this type of behaviour can be prevented. It is probably true to say that bullies usually work in groups with a 'leader' and children tend to become crueller when in numbers.

Bullies are often hostile and aggressive people who feel inadequate and are unable to cope with their own problems. By picking on someone who appears weaker than themselves and causing them distress they make themselves feel more powerful and in control. However, it must also be said that some children bully because they have no conception that they should limit their demands and, whilst again this is no excuse for their behaviour, it goes some way to explaining their forceful nature to get what they want.

Varying backgrounds and upbringings

The difficulty arises when a child turns out to be a bully despite very different backgrounds and family upbringings. A child who is the typical 'spoilt brat' who has been indulged and had their every whim pandered to is just as likely to make excessive demands on others as a child who has never been indulged and who has subsequently learned that intimidation of others is a way of making themselves feel powerful and that they can often get what they want through this type of behaviour. There is then no real 'pattern' as to why a child turns out to be a bully, although lack of respect for others appears to be one of the main reasons.

 ◆ TIP ◆

Teach your child to respect others from a young age. Ensure that they are aware that being judgemental and resorting to bullying tactics is not acceptable behaviour.

Victims becoming bullies

It should be expected that a child who has experienced how hurtful and distressing it can be to be bullied would never resort to this type of behaviour themselves. This is untrue as some bullies are essentially 'victims-turned-bullies' who, for many reasons, have turned the tables and become the hunter rather than the prey. You would think that a victim who has suffered at the hands of a bully would have more compassion, and having felt the pain and anguish themselves, could never resort to inflicting such distress on others. However sometimes victims decide that it is 'pay back time' and sometimes they simply get fed up of being picked on and decide that the time is right for them to be the bully.

Bullying when part of a group

Often a bully who is part of a group will be the strongest of the participants, with 'followers' who are probably a lot weaker than themselves and reluctant to stand up to the group leader. Most children who are part of this kind of group want to be liked and accepted and will often go along with other group members, albeit reluctantly, as they feel powerless to object for fear of rejection and being ostracized themselves. Going along with the bullying, even reluctantly, is in their eyes, better than risking being bullied themselves.

HOW TO HELP YOUR CHILD IF THEY ARE DOING THE BULLYING

It is all well and done for parents and teachers to offer help, reassurance and advice to a child who is being bullied and, chances are, everyone's sympathies will lie with the victim. However, without wishing to distract in any way from the suffering of the victim, it is probably true to say that the bully themselves needs as much, and sometimes even more, help and encouragement.

Why do children resort to bullying? For sure, bullying is not a likeable trait or a behaviour worthy of praise. However it is very common in both children and adults who feel that they have better means of getting what they want through issuing threats and violence rather than by establishing friendships and compromising. For this reason alone we must assume that bullies need help.

Remain calm

It is most important that you remain calm if you discover that your child is bullying another. You may feel resentment and anger towards your child for the apparent suffering they are putting another individual through. If the victim's parents have contacted you about your child's behaviour you may feel embarrassed, shocked and defensive. However, it is paramount that you control your feelings and deal with the situation in a rational way. After all losing your temper, shouting or physically punishing your child for their behaviour gives out the very messages that you are yourself trying to avoid and tells your child – the bully – that intimidation is acceptable.

HELPING YOUR CHILD IF THEY ARE RESORTING TO BULLYING OTHERS:

◆ Talk to your child and ask them why they feel the need to bully. Find out whether something is troubling them as this may be triggering their need to bully others.

◆ Reassure your child that, despite their behaviour, you still love them. They need to know that it is their behaviour you dislike and not them.

◆ Reassure your child that you will work with them in order to help them to change their behaviour.

◆ Teach your child the difference between assertiveness and aggression – see page 70 for more information.

◆ Encourage your child to find a way of making amends to their victims.

◆ Talk to the staff at your child's school and explain that you are working with your child to put a stop to their unacceptable behaviour.

◆ Praise your child when they have managed to control their temper.

Although no-one wants to believe the worst in their child and many of us would find it incomprehensible that our child can enjoy making another suffer in this way, it has to be acknowledged that children do not always behave in a manner that we would be proud of and ignoring your child's behaviour when they are clearly making another child's life a misery is simply not acceptable.

Talking to your child

Usually a bully will feel worthless, just as they are trying to make their victims feel, and by making someone else unhappy and getting them to be laughed at and ridiculed they are in effect making themselves feel popular and important. As a parent of a child who feels the need to resort to bullying others you will need to find out why their self-confidence is at such a low ebb, making them feel the need to behave in such a manner.

Helping your child control their feelings

Most bullies work in gangs and it is their followers that they are initially trying to impress in order to gain a higher standing within the group and carve out their position at the head of the group – they want to be 'top dog' and are prepared to use violence and aggression in order to command the obedience and loyalty of others.

Bullies need help to build their self-esteem and confidence in a constructive manner. They need some direction and focus in their lives and will ultimately need to talk to someone about their feelings, why they are prone to such anger and aggression. Bullies need to learn how to control their temper and channel their anger constructively and must learn the importance of making meaningful friendships whereby they learn to get along with their peers rather than feel the need to control them.

HOW CAN CHILDREN AND THEIR PARENTS COPE WITH BULLYING?

Firstly, and most importantly, children need to be believed. If your child or indeed someone else's child, tells you that they are being victimized then you must take them seriously. Listen to what they have to say and respond to what they are telling you. It may only be a very slight form of bullying, such as name calling, but, to a child, this can be very upsetting and, if it occurs over a prolonged period of time can, be very distressing and damaging.

A child who is being bullied will feel better just by having someone to open up and talk to. Although telling someone about the problem will not automatically make it go away, it is the first very big step to getting it sorted and it is often very difficult for a child to do. If, when they have plucked up the courage to tell you about their suffering, you do not respond to their plight or ignore how much it is affecting them then they will feel completely let down and extremely vulnerable.

DEALING WITH BULLYING IN SCHOOL:

◆ As soon as you learn that your child is being bullied keep a diary of incidents. Include notes and photographs of any injuries sustained and any doctor or hospital appointments made as a result of the bullying.

◆ Speak to your child's form teacher initially. Never lose your temper or shout no matter how distressed, angry or upset you are.

◆ If after speaking to your child's form teacher the bullying continues, then take your complaint to the Head of Year. Ask for a meeting and request an investigation into the bullying.

◆ If your child continues to be bullied, make an appointment to see the head teacher and request to see the school's Discipline or Anti-bullying Policy – all schools must have one in place.

◆ Finally, the Board of Governors or your Local Authority can be contacted if all else fails.

SCHOOLS AND BULLYING

Schools are obliged to deal with any incidents of bullying. They must do the following.

◆ Take the matter seriously and investigate the incidents.

◆ Interview the victim.

◆ Interview the bully.

◆ Decide on appropriate action. This may include obtaining an apology, imposing sanctions, holding lessons to highlight the distress caused by bullying, providing support for the victim etc.

◆ Follow up their investigation by having a meeting with the victim's parents to report the outcome and the action taken.

◆ Hold written records of the incident, interviews and action.

PRACTISING SELF-ASSERTIVENESS

Practising some basic self-assertiveness skills can be beneficial to both bullies and their victims. Being self-assertive can help a child to feel good about themselves and gives them a sense of well being.

Aggressive vs. assertive

Assertiveness is *not* the same as aggression. Most people will fall into one of three categories:

1. **Passive** These people are of the opinion that other people's rights matter more than their own. They usually lack self-esteem and confidence.

2. **Assertive** These people respect both themselves and others equally.

3. **Aggressive** These people behave as if their rights are more important than the rights of others.

Broadly speaking a bully will fall into the 'aggressive' category whilst their victim will fall into the 'passive' category.

ENCOURAGING ASSERTIVENESS

In order for your child to practise being assertive you will need to encourage them to do the following.

◆ Know their own mind and be clear about what they want.

◆ Be prepared for all eventualities – plan ahead and prepare their response.

◆ Learn how to say 'no' and mean it. If they are not happy with a certain situation they should not be pressured into giving in but should learn to stand firm.

◆ Avoid arguments.

- Avoid getting angry and upset.

- Don't make excuses for bad behaviour – where possible, offer alternatives or suggest a compromise.

Remember that by being assertive and saying 'no' to someone's request, you are not rejecting that person you are simply refusing a request.

HELP AND ADVICE ON WHAT TO DO ABOUT BULLYING

The Kidscape website, www.kidscape.org.uk, has lots of practical suggestions of what to do about bullying. The website has a useful information sheet, titled *Assertiveness for Children*, which sets out the basic outlines for human rights and gives practical guidance and techniques for children to become more assertive and thereby reduce the chances of them becoming victims of bullying.

In addition to Kidscape you may find it helpful to contact the following organizations for help and advice on bullying:

www.bullying.co.uk – Bullying UK offers help and advice for both parents and children dealing with school bullying.

www.dfes.gov.uk/bullying – the Department for Children, Schools and Families has information on their website about tackling bullying in schools and concentrates in particular on cyberbullying.

5

DANGERS ONLINE

In an age where the use of technology is widespread and where even the youngest of children are computer literate, it has to be said that today's children face more dangers than they did perhaps ten or twenty years ago. The internet, though useful if used correctly, poses a great threat to our children if they are left unchecked whilst online and allowed to access unsuitable material. Dangers from chat rooms, unheard of only a relatively short time ago, now pose a real threat of danger to our children.

TAKING RESPONSIBILITY FOR YOUR CHILD'S INTERNET USE

Parents who are ignorant of the internet and who are unaware of how it works can not be excused when it comes to protecting their child. The simple answer, therefore, is that all parents who own a computer or who allow their child to access the internet are responsible for the material they view. As such, if you are not computer literate but allow your child access to the internet perhaps now is the time to take a look at the internet. Find out how you can ensure that your child is safe whilst online and what you can do to minimise any risks to them.

CHAT ROOMS

There have been many reports about the dangers of the internet, however, it is probably true to say that the biggest threat to our children today are 'chat rooms'. Many children access chat rooms on a regular basis without ever encountering a problem. It is important that whilst we are not lax in our responsibility towards our children when it comes to the internet neither should we become hysterical at the first signs that our children are taking an interest in the internet.

Parents need to be aware of the following:

◆ What chat rooms are.

◆ How they can be dangerous.

◆ How to minimize any risks to their child.

What is a chat room?

A chat room is an online forum where people can chat online to other people. Individuals can chat on a one-to-one basis or in a themed room with several other people.

In a chat room it is possible to do the following.

◆ Create personal profiles.

◆ Hold private conversations.

◆ Play games.

◆ Hold discussions on any number of topics.

Although, if used correctly, chat rooms can be a fun way of making friends and getting to know people over the internet, the dangers begin to surface when things move on from the chat room to email, telephone conversations and then, finally, face-to-face meetings. This may involve a child unwittingly arranging to meet someone whom they genuinely believe to be of like mind and age but whom may, in reality, turn out to be a predator intent on causing the child harm.

SPOTTING AN ONLINE PREDATOR

It is often very difficult to spot an online predator largely due to the fact that they rarely proposition a child early on. They start by getting to know the child, building up a relationship, allowing the child to put their trust in them and then, once the child thinks they have found a friend they can rely on, the predator moves in to sexually proposition them. The whole situation is processed gradually and often vulnerable children are targeted; the ones who do not appear to say very much in the chat room and those who appear to readily express agreement. The predator is hoping that the quieter, more reserved participants are more likely to be lonely and looking for attention and these are the children who are more likely to be targeted. Often, by the time the predator has arranged to meet the child, they have already succumbed to their charms and they are then more likely to trust the person and submit to their advances.

SETTING GROUND RULES FOR INTERNET USE

Despite the very real dangers we must not forget that the internet is a very useful tool which can open up a whole new world of information for our children. It is a quick way for young people to find information, help them to study and, of course, keep in touch with their friends as well as meeting new ones.

Parents must however bear in mind that the internet is also an easy tool for child abuse and fraud. Using the internet appropriately and sensibly will not cause problems, however overuse of the internet is both addictive and unhealthy and it is important that parents supervise their children closely whilst they are using it.

Think about setting some ground rules if you are intending to allow your child to use the internet so that you can be sure that they are safe online.

SAFETY CHECKLIST FOR USING THE INTERNET

✓ Learn about computers and chat rooms yourself. Try out a chat room and see how they work so that you will be able to completely understand what your child is getting into.

✓ Visit the websites your child uses to make sure that they are suitable.

✓ Make sure that you discuss which sites you are happy for your child to browse and which are off limits.

✓ Put the computer in a 'family room' rather than allowing your child to have one in their bedroom. This way you can supervise them whilst they are online. Make sure the monitor faces outwards so that you can see, at all times, what is on the screen.

✓ Invest in software filters which block access to unsuitable websites and those with sexual content. However, be aware that these filters do not totally ensure that internet use is safe and you must still take an active interest in the sites your child is using.

✓ Limit the amount of time your child spends on the internet. Spending too much time online is unhealthy and can become addictive. Don't allow your child to persuade you to let them have an 'extra half an hour'. Decide on a suitable length of time and stick to it. Never be tempted to allow them to stay online for prolonged lengths of time because it is 'keeping them quiet'.

✓ Make sure that your child tells you if someone is asking them unsuitable questions or trying to glean information they are unhappy divulging.

✓ Make sure that your child is completely aware of the dangers posed by the internet and they never reveal their real name, address, home or mobile telephone numbers or any other personal details.

✓ Never allow your child to post photographs of themselves on the internet.

✓ Never allow your child to arrange to meet someone they have been in contact with over the internet.

Making your child aware of the importance of grounds rules

Although you should not resort to scare tactics when it comes to allowing your child to use the internet it is important that they understand the importance of abiding by your rules and they are aware that not all people are genuine and can be trusted. Make sure that your child understands that, because they can't actually 'see' the person they are in contact with over the internet, there is a possibility that the person is not actually who they are pretending to be. Many paedophiles pose as children to gain trust prior to arranging to meet someone in person.

◆ FACT ◆

Strangers on the internet can be just as dangerous as those on the street and children and teenagers need to be aware of these dangers.

Ensure that you are available for your child should they need to talk to you and that they are aware that you are willing and able to help them if they are concerned about something they have encountered online.

Your child should inform you immediately if they encounter someone who is asking them questions which make them feel uncomfortable or uneasy. Make sure that you discuss your ground rules with your child and, before allowing them access to the internet, ensure that they understand and agree to abide by these rules.

WARNING SIGNS

There may be times when your child is unable or unwilling to open up to you. Perhaps they are afraid that you will put a stop to them using the internet or they may simply think they are mature enough and wise enough to handle any problem themselves. It is important to remember that children who have not openly discussed any

potential problems with you may still be giving out 'warning signs'
As a parent you need to be aware of these signs as they may point
to the fact that your child is developing problems whilst using the
internet.

You should be concerned if your child does the following.

♦ Spends an unhealthy number of hours logged on.

♦ Becomes secretive when using the computer.

♦ Suddenly starts to take more interest in sexual matters or starts
to ask questions relating to sexual matters.

♦ Starts to have trouble sleeping.

♦ Begins to change their usual routine for no apparent reason.

♦ Starts arranging to meet people and are reluctant to tell you
where they are going or who they are going with.

If you notice any of the above signs you should consider whether or
not the internet has anything to do with your child's change in
behaviour. Look at their emails and ask them questions about their
use of the internet to get to the bottom of their behaviour.

HELP AND ADVICE ON HOW TO USE THE INTERNET SAFELY

www.pin.org.uk – The Parent Information Network contains useful
information about using the internet safely.

6

THE LEGAL FRAMEWORK FOR PROTECTING CHILDREN FROM ABUSE

UNDERSTANDING YOUR CHILD'S LEGAL RIGHTS

Very few parents have a clear understanding of their child's legal rights assuming that they have sole 'powers' over them and can decide, without intervention, how best to bring up their own children. In the main this is true. Responsible parents, who have only the best interests of their children at heart, will have no problems.

Whereas once the responsibility for choosing the right childcare for their child or administering discipline or punishment, for example, lay strictly with the parents, these areas of parenting are no longer seen as simply a private family choice and they are governed by legislation.

Today, the view that parents can no longer simply care for their children as they please is now firmly established and, whilst parents have a considerable amount of flexibility when it comes to deciding how to raise their children, there are now laws in place to deal with issues such as abuse and neglect. It is important to understand the legal framework which is in place to ensure the protection of children.

THE RELEVANT LAWS FOR PROTECTION OF CHILDREN

The legal framework for the care and protection of children in the United Kingdom was passed during the 1980s and 1990s. The laws which are relevant are the following.

◆ *The Children Act 1989.* This applies to England and Wales.

◆ *The Children Act 1995.* This applies to Scotland.

◆ *The Children Order 1996.* This applies to Northern Ireland.

Each of the aforementioned laws are primary legislation which means they lay out the details of the law in legal language. However, they do not fully explain how child protection works in daily practice. Therefore this legislation is supported further by guidance issued by national government departments. Local guidance documents are drafted by local child protection committees and parents and carers would need to consult their own local procedures or guidance should the need arise.

THE CHILDREN ACT 1989

The Children Act 1989 came into force on 14th October 1991. This Act has had a major impact on the law which relates to children and it affects all children and their families.

Parental responsibility

The Children Act 1989 puts the emphasis on the fact that parents should have responsibilities for their children, rather than rights over them. In the case of *The Children Act 1989,* parental responsibility is defined as the rights, duties, powers, responsibilities and authority that, by law, a parent of a child has in relation to the child and to their property.

The Children Act 1989 acknowledges the importance of the wishes of the child and recognizes that parental responsibility is an important concept when deciding who is in a position to make decisions about the child, and who should be contacted in the case of any legal proceedings.

WHO HOLDS PARENTAL RESPONSIBILITY?

The Children Act 1989 concluded that those who can hold parental responsibility are the following.

◆ The child's natural parents. The mother of the child holds parental responsibility for her child regardless of whether she is married or not. A mother can only lose her right to parental responsibility when an adoption or freeing order is made. The *natural* father of the child has joint parental responsibility with the natural mother if they are married to each other at the time of the child's birth, or if they subsequently marry. The child's natural father can only lose parental responsibility if an adoption or freeing order is made.

◆ The unmarried father can share equal parental responsibility with the child's mother if both parents register the birth of the baby together. The law was changed on 1 December 2003 to make it easier for unmarried fathers to obtain equal parental responsibility for their children. This change in the law does not apply to births registered prior to 1 December 2003. Until the change in the law, unmarried fathers, unlike mothers and married fathers, did not have automatic parental responsibility for their child. Unmarried fathers can also obtain parental responsibility by marrying the child's mother, signing an official agreement with the child's mother or obtaining a court order.

◆ The step-parent can acquire parental responsibility by obtaining a residence order, however they will lose parental responsibility if that order ends.

◆ The local authority can acquire parental responsibility if they obtain a care order or emergency protection order, however they will lose it when that order ends.

◆ Others, such as grandparents, may acquire parental responsibility in some cases if they acquire it by court order and, once again, they will lose it when the order ends.

What parental responsibility entails

Parental responsibility allows the adult to be involved in decisions such as where the child lives, how they are educated, what religion they will follow and what medical treatment they are allowed to receive. Without parental responsibility you have no rights in any of these decisions. Parental responsibility ceases to apply once a child reaches the age of 18 years. Although parental responsibility may be shared it cannot be transferred or surrendered. Each person who is responsible for a child can act alone and exercise their responsibility. That said, they are not allowed to do this in any way which may be incompatible with a court order made under the 1989 Act.

Principles dictating practice

The Children Act 1989 sets out a series of principles which dictate practice and procedure in and out of court such as:

◆ Children are generally better off being looked after by their families.

◆ Parents and guardians retain parental responsibility and work together with the local authority.

◆ Court orders should not be made unless it is considered that this is better than making no order at all.

◆ The child's welfare is the court's paramount consideration at all times.

◆ A court order is necessary before the local authority can acquire parental responsibility.

◆ Orders are available to protect children and to avoid unwarranted intervention in family life.

FACT

Children are not the possessions of their parents. Although parents are responsible for their children they do not have absolute rights over them.

7

ABUSE OF CHILDREN WITH DISABILITIES

As the parent of a child with a disability it is highly likely that you will already be very protective of them. Depending on the severity of your child's disability you may constantly worry about their safety. The added pressure you may be under when faced with the prospect of caring for a child with disabilities, coupled with the realization that your disabled child may be more vulnerable to abuse can be quite terrifying.

Although all children are vulnerable, those with a disability are more at risk either through their inability to understand the dangers they are faced with or by not being able to communicate adequately when something is not right.

PICKING UP ON WORRYING BEHAVIOUR

Some children with learning disabilities may behave in a much younger way than their actual age, and this may in turn mean that they are less aware of the boundaries between public and private behaviour. As a parent of a disabled child you will need to support your child as they learn. In doing so however, you should never be too quick to dismiss any worrying behaviour they may show as an inevitable consequence of their disability. Always ask yourself if you would be concerned about their behaviour if your child did not have a disability rather than use their disability to explain away their behaviour.

WHY DISABLED CHILDREN ARE MORE AT RISK FROM ABUSE

As I have just mentioned, a child with a disability is no less likely to be abused that any other child and, unfortunately, sometimes they are more at risk from abuse.

Disabled children can be more at risk for a number of reasons.

◆ A disabled child may need more personal physical care because of their disabilities and this care may be required to go on much longer than if they were not disabled. It is, of course, perfectly possible to administer personal physical care to a disabled child with respect and consideration but sadly, disabled children may experience abuse through poor standards in their care or by suffering directly from their need for assistance.

◆ Sometimes it is difficult for disabled children to understand and appreciate when abusive behaviour is being directed towards them. This may be because they have been subjected to continual, intrusive medical procedures due to their condition. Having become accustomed to these procedures they may be unable to differentiate between when they are being exploited and these intrusive procedures. Sometimes their own sense of dignity is distorted.

◆ A child with a learning or communication difficulty may have a problem expressing themselves. They may not be able to tell a person they trust what they are experiencing.

◆ Disabled children with a high level of disability may be completely unable to resist their abuser and may have no way of preventing the abuse from taking place.

◆ Parents of a disabled child may feel isolated. Lack of support and exhaustion can sometimes contribute to them physically hurting their child themselves through relentless pressure and sheer frustration. Often a disabled child will need constant care, 24 hours a day, seven days a week. This places an enormous responsibility on their shoulders often resulting in the parents' inability to cope.

◆ Disabled children are at risk from abuse if they have a high number of different carers. If they are unable to differentiate between necessary and inappropriate intrusive attention they may begin to think that *all* intrusive attention is normal and necessary making them very vulnerable to abuse.

PRIORITIZING YOUR CHILD'S PREFERENCES

As parents of a disabled child you should keep your child's preferences in the forefront of your mind at all times. Even if your child finds it difficult to express themselves you must always respect their privacy and dignity and make sure that any carers they are in contact with do the same. Keep a close eye on any medical procedures which are carried out on your child and ensure that you and your child are responsible for the overall care they receive.

◆ **FACT** ◆

Always treat your child with the dignity and respect they deserve. Make sure that any other carers do the same and that they take into account your child's preferences. Being disabled does not mean that a child is devoid of feelings and embarrassment.

Encourage your child to take as much responsibility for their own care as possible. Make sure that they are aware that only a certain number of people are expected to take care of their intimate needs so that they do not come to believe that these needs may be met by anyone.

WHAT KIND OF ABUSE MIGHT DISABLED CHILDREN ENCOUNTER?

Unfortunately disabled children are one of the most vulnerable groups of people in our society. Disabled children are between two and four times more likely to be abused than other children, and, as such, they need to be protected. Disabled children are often unable to communicate adequately or express themselves in a way that highlights their suffering and, as a consequence, sometimes the abuse can go on for years. Although a disabled child may be unable to speak up for themselves and ask for help we must never forget that the trauma and suffering they experience will be just as damaging for them as for any other child.

Living away from home

Disabled children living away from home, who lack the presence of a parent or other trusted adult, are much more vulnerable to abuse. Parents may be fearful of complaining in case their child ends up losing the specialist care they so desperately need and children may find it difficult to complain or may be reluctant to do so for fear of reprimand or punishment.

Institutions which care for disabled children are often governed by firm, fixed routines. Mealtimes and bedtimes, for example will be set, leaving very little flexibility and children will have little or no opportunity to learn assertiveness or to make choices. Ultimately they may end up believing there is no point in making a fuss or questioning how things are done and, over time, they will come to accept this as a way of life.

Types of abuse

These are some of the ways in which a disabled child may be abused.

- ◆ Being force fed
- ◆ Being isolated
- ◆ Being made to carry out their toileting needs in public
- ◆ Being over sedated
- ◆ Being physically restrained
- ◆ Confined to a room or bed

- Discrimination
- Lack of privacy
- Segregated
- Sexual abuse.

SIGNS OF ABUSE IN DISABLED CHILDREN

It can often be much harder to spot the signs of abuse in disabled children as sometimes changes in behaviour and mood swings tend to be put down to the child's disability rather than a need for the carers to look closer.

As a parent you will of course know your child well and if you notice any of the following signs you should be concerned.

- Eating problems which result in fluctuations in weight.
- Inappropriate sexual behaviour or awareness.
- Reluctance to socialize with or go near a particular adult.
- Self-harming.
- Sleep problems.
- Unexpected fear of a particular adult.
- Unexplained or repeated injuries or bruising.
- Unusual aggressive behaviour.
- Unusual withdrawn behaviour.

HOW YOU CAN HELP YOUR DISABLED CHILD TO KEEP SAFE

Parents of disabled children are usually instinctively more protective of them than parents with an able-bodied child and this may be because they are already aware of how vulnerable to abuse they are.

It is probably true to say that most people find it incomprehensible and abhorrent that someone would want to abuse a disabled child, however this does not alter the fact that it does happen.

You can help to ensure that your child is safe and protected by doing the following.

◆ Reassure yourself that your child is happy and comfortable with any carers they are in contact with. This is very important if the carer has to provide your child with intimate care.

◆ Never underestimate your child's feelings. Listen carefully to everything they tell you and always take them seriously.

◆ Ask questions. Be happy in your own mind that the care and medical treatment your child receives takes into account both the wishes of your child and yourself. If you are unsure about anything ask for an explanation.

◆ If your child receives care outside of the home, ask to see the settings policies and procedures on child protection. Enquire how staff are vetted, meet the staff who will be responsible for your child's care and ask questions. Remember that many abusers will seek jobs which bring them into contact with children, particularly if the contact is unsupervised.

◆ Make sure that your child can communicate with you about any situations they are unhappy with. If your child has speech problems then the use of pictures and images may help to maximize your communication with them.

SAFETY CHECKLIST FOR DEALING WITH ABUSE

It is absolutely paramount that all children, and disabled children are no exception, are taught the importance of how to stay safe.

We can do this by:

✓ Helping them to understand exactly what abusive behaviour is.

✓ Teaching them to respect their own bodies.

✓ Encouraging them to tell someone how they are feeling.

✓ Ensuring that they are not afraid to speak out if someone acts inappropriately towards them.

✓ Helping them to understand what constitutes danger, and how to avoid it.

✓ Ensuring they know how to summon help if necessary.

EMPOWERING YOUR CHILD

Encouraging our children to be responsible for themselves is a way of 'empowering' them. Allow your child to make choices, even if those choices may not always be the right ones. Respecting their likes, dislikes and feelings will help your child to discover themselves and to feel happy with who they are. Ask your child about their preferences and opinions and include them in decision making.

ENCOURAGING POSITIVE IMAGES OF DISABLED PEOPLE

Quite often disabled children will feel inadequate and get downhearted. It is important, as a parent, that you reiterate often how much you love your child. Never allow their disability to cloud your judgement and make sure that you praise your child for the things they can do well. Make your child feel good about themselves and no matter how big or small their achievements are, let them know how proud you are of them.

Encouraging positive images of disabled people in your home will be an enormous confidence boost to your child who will love to look at pictures of models, sports men and women, politicians, teachers, musicians and entertainers who have a disability just like them. These positive images will help to reinforce that they can be successful and achieve high goals despite their disability.

8

PHYSICAL ABUSE

WHAT IS PHYSICAL ABUSE?

Physical abuse is when a child has been intentionally inflicted with an injury. It can sometimes be quite difficult to recognize whether a child has suffered from a particular injury accidentally, such as through a fall; or intentionally such as being hit or kicked. If a child is too young to be able to speak or if they suffer from a disability which affects their communication skills this situation can be all the more difficult to determine.

Types of physical abuse

Physical abuse can take on many forms including the following.

◆ Being bitten.

◆ Being deliberately burned or scalded.

◆ Being frightened – this could mean forcing a child into a dark space or cupboard.

◆ Being hit with hands, fists or implements.

◆ Being kicked.

◆ Being poisoned – inappropriate use of alcohol, drugs, prescription medicine or household substances.

◆ Being pushed or shoved.

◆ Being shaken.

◆ Being squeezed.

◆ Being suffocated.

Although physical abuse usually results in obvious injury, it is also damaging to children emotionally and socially. Often this pain will last long after any bruises and wounds have healed. The longer the physical abuse of a child occurs, the more serious the impact, and abuse of this kind can lead to bruising, cuts, burns, fractures, internal injuries and, in the most extreme cases, even death.

Immediate consequences of physical abuse

One of the most disturbing aspects of physical abuse which cannot be ignored is the *stress* it puts on the child. Exposure to violence, injury and trauma on a regular basis causes the victim to become stressed which can result in permanent problems such as becoming emotionally numb, craving high-risk dangerous experiences and self-harming.

The following are just some of the immediate effects which may be experienced by a child suffering from physical abuse:

◆ Aggressive behaviour towards others

◆ Anxiety and stress

◆ Attention problems

◆ Academic difficulties

◆ Concentration difficulties

◆ Fear

◆ Shyness

◆ Failure to make friends

◆ Bed wetting

◆ Behaviour problems

- Stuttering

- Truancy – particularly in the case of bullying

- Depression

- Running away

- Withdrawing from physical contact.

It is paramount that children know that they can talk to their parents, that what they tell them is taken seriously and, if necessary, it will be acted upon. As a parent we all want what is best for our children however, sometimes a child's anxieties and fears are pushed to one side by those who love them the most for fear of creating unnecessary problems. There are some parents who harbour the notion that 'ignoring a problem will make it go away' although this attitude of burying the head in the sand may be taken with the child's welfare at heart it is a very dangerous route to take. By confiding in you, your child has expressed a need for help. They may wait until they feel they can no longer cope with things as they are or they may open up to you from the very first instance. However what they tell you must be acted upon immediately.

LONG-TERM CONSEQUENCES OF PHYSICAL ABUSE

Children are often powerless to prevent abuse, particularly if they are too young to tell someone what they are experiencing. They end up blaming themselves for what is happening and begin to feel worthless and deserving of the 'punishment'. They will start to develop a range of maladaptive, self-destructive and anti-social behaviours to try to cope with what is happening to them. Even children who are old enough to communicate often keep the abuse a 'secret' particularly if they are suffering at the hands of a family member or friend. They may have been threatened by the abuser or made to feel that the abuse is a direct result of their own behaviour. This can have a life-long effect on the child and result in them having problems forging relationships in later life.

A child who is led to believe that the abuse they are suffering is a direct response to their own behaviour will become withdrawn and afraid of trying out new experiences for fear of 'failure' and risk of further punishment. Their curiosity will wane and the child may never achieve their full intellectual potential.

CHOOSING THE RIGHT CHILDCARE

There have been reports in the press recently highlighting physical abuse inflicted on children by their carers. The carers in question have been nannies, childminders or nursery assistants. Parents must ensure that they only choose registered childcare if they are intending leaving their children with someone else, perhaps to return to work.

Although choosing a registered childcare provider will not eliminate all risks, you can be confident that the provider has been inspected by the Office for Standards in Care and Education (Ofsted), the governing body for England. They will have had their setting inspected and the carer themselves will have undertaken a criminal records bureau check to ensure that they are deemed suitable to be working with young children. Quite simply, employing an unregistered childcare provider is both illegal and potentially dangerous to your child.

Although physical injuries are common in children and a child who appears to have a history of age-appropriate injuries should not automatically raise suspicion of child abuse, it is important for parents who leave their children in the care of a nanny, childminder or nursery setting to be aware of any warning signs of physical abuse such as:

◆ Varying injuries sustained over a period of time – for example, bruises of differing colour would imply that a child has been subjected to injury over a period of time.

◆ Illnesses which cannot be accounted for such as recurring stomach pains or headaches.

◆ Appearing to succumb to more than an average amount of accidents for which there is no explanation for the injury.

Obviously, if your child is coming home from the childcare setting with an injury, you should be informed by the practitioner of how this has been sustained. Even the most vigilant of practitioners will be unable to prevent every knock or fall. It is important, if your child is suffering from regular injuries, to ascertain whether these may be sustained as a result of neglect or abuse. No-one likes to think that children are not being cared for adequately but sometimes this is the case. If your child appears to be suffering from injuries which are not usual given their age or ability, for example, broken bones in a child who is too young to walk or climb, then your suspicions should be aroused and questions need to be asked.

Other types of childcare

Although it is impossible to be with your child 24 hours a day, seven days a week, particularly as they get older, it is our duty as parents to ensure that the people we trust the care of our children with are suitable. Never has this been more apparent than when choosing a babysitter.

Choosing a babysitter

Babysitters advertise their services in newspapers, on noticeboards and in shop windows however, is this really the way you should be seeking childcare for your baby or young child? No-one should employ a babysitter they do not know well. Trusting a family member or friend with the care of your child is not completely risk free of course, however it is much more preferable to answering the advertisement of a total stranger. Always remember that abusers know how to find their victims and endearing themselves to a family by offering their services as a babysitter is one way for them to find their victims.

Vetting holiday clubs

Holiday clubs, both abroad and in the United Kingdom, should also be vetted carefully. Often parents have no idea who they are leaving their children with in these kinds of clubs. If the staff are only employed as casual labour for the holiday season it is much more likely that they have not undergone important checks. The high volume of children being left in holiday clubs, perhaps only for the duration of a week or two, make it much easier for abusers to select their victims and for them to cover up any abuse.

You can vet holiday clubs by doing the following.

◆ Asking to see evidence of staff training and first aid qualifications.

◆ Asking to see evidence of police checks on staff.

◆ Requesting information on safety procedures.

◆ Requesting information on the collection of children (how are staff made aware of who is responsible for collecting a child?)

◆ Checking the club's equipment and premises prior to leaving your child.

◆ Choose a well established holiday company with a good reputation.

REDUCING THE RISK OF ACCIDENTS

All children will sustain accidental injuries in the course of daily activities and play and this is all part of growing up and exploring. However it is the job of the parents and practitioners to eliminate potential dangers as much as possible – there is more about safety in the home and garden earlier in Chapters 1 and 2.

◆ **FACT** ◆

Cases of child abuse generally arise within the family, but there have been instances when childcare practitioners or teachers have been responsible for inflicting abuse on children. Therefore it is paramount that parents are vigilant when it comes to choosing childcare.

HOW TO PROTECT YOUR CHILD FROM PHYSICAL ABUSE

Physical abuse can happen to any child in any family set up. Children can suffer this kind of abuse from their immediate families, childcare workers, babysitters or friends and it is vital that parents are aware of the signs of physical abuse in order to protect their children.

Signs of physical abuse

◆ Aggression

◆ Bite marks

◆ Burns or scalds

◆ Delayed development

◆ Frequent broken bones

◆ Frequent, unexplained injuries such as bruises, cuts and grazes

◆ Lack of appetite

◆ Lack of interest in surroundings and activities

◆ Lack of self-esteem.

Recognizing the signs of physical abuse is the first step to protecting your child. If you are aware of the signs and symptoms it will be much easier for you to deal with any issues should they arise. A child may suffer physical abuse at home, in daycare or at school in the form of bullying. There is more on bullying and how to deal with it in Chapter 4.

Noticing the signs

Young children who find it difficult to communicate their feelings or indeed those who are not of the age to verbally communicate are the most vulnerable when it comes to any form of abuse as, quite often, this is why they have been 'chosen' by the abuser who will feel 'safe' that their victim is unable to communicate what is happening to them. Parents and carers should be concerned if their child shows any of the signs mentioned previously along with regular injuries which cannot be explained.

Accidential injuries

Broadly speaking injuries to the following parts of the body may be seen as **accidental**.

- Forehead
- Chin
- Nose
- Knees
- Elbows
- Forearms
- Spine
- Hips
- Shins.

Non-accidental injuries

The following areas are common sites for **non-accidental** injuries.

- Lips and mouth
- Eyes
- Ears
- Cheeks
- Skull
- Chest
- Stomach

- ◆ Buttocks
- ◆ Back of legs
- ◆ Upper and inner arms
- ◆ Genital areas
- ◆ Rectal areas
- ◆ Soles of the feet
- ◆ Neck.

It is very rare for a child to sustain an accidental injury to the neck. Equally, a torn Frenulum (the tongue attachment) should be viewed with suspicion. Haemorrhages to the earlobes are also rarely accidental as are *two* black eyes, particularly if there are no other apparent injuries to the head or face.

Physical abuse to a child may not always be a result of deliberate cruelty. Sometimes an adult, even a parent, can lose control, snap and inflict this kind of abuse.

CAUSE FOR CONCERN

A child who is being subjected to physical abuse may show a considerable change in their behaviour. As a parent you will, of course, know your child well and a child's pattern of behaviour can vary considerably depending on their age and stage of development therefore these factors must be taken into account when deciding whether any abuse has taken place.

As a parent some of the signs which should concern you are the following.

- ◆ Withdrawing from physical contact – often a child who has been struck will shy away from physical contact for fear or repercussion.

- Withdrawing from close relationships with adults or children – children who have trusted someone who has then gone on to abuse them will be reluctant to put themselves in that position again and will shy away from forging friendships.

- Showing apprehension when other children cry – often children feel the suffering of others and a child who has been abused may see another child who is showing distress as suffering in the same way as themselves.

- Showing fear of certain adults – a child who is being abused may be frightened to tell someone about their suffering. They may have been threatened by their abuser or have fear of repercussions. However despite their silence, they will be reluctant to go near their abuser and may well show their fear without actually meaning to.

- Refusing to leave home/expressing a wish not to go somewhere – a child who is being abused outside the home will be reluctant to leave the safety of their home. If your child expresses a sincere wish not to attend a certain club, childcare setting, class etc., investigate the reason for their reluctance.

- Being unable to explain their injuries – if your child has an injury and is reluctant to discuss it with you or cannot give you a satisfactory explanation of how it came about then you should be concerned.

- Displaying frozen awareness – a child who is constantly watchful when a certain adult is around them may be showing fear of abuse.

- Running away from home – children who suddenly start to run away from home may be trying to escape the fear they are suffering.

- Displaying changes in their eating patterns – overeating or refusal to eat are both signs of distress and unhappiness.

If your child displays any of the above characteristics or if they attempt to tell you about something which is worrying them in a 'covert' manner then you should take them seriously. Often children will express their feelings when playing, for example, during role play or when they are being creative. Paintings and drawings may be an outlet for their fear and frustration.

9

EMOTIONAL ABUSE

WHAT IS EMOTIONAL ABUSE?

Emotional abuse is when a child is refused love, approval and acceptance. Emotional abuse can be in the form of the following.

- ◆ Being blamed for things which are not the child's fault

- ◆ Being made to feel inadequate and unworthy of love and affection

- ◆ Being ridiculed

- ◆ Being shouted at

- ◆ Being sworn at

- ◆ Being threatened

- ◆ Being constantly criticised

- ◆ Feeling in danger or frightened.

◆ FACT ◆

Whether a child is being sexually, physically or emotionally abused or whether they are suffering from neglect they will all experience some form of emotional suffering. Therefore it is reasonable to say that emotional abuse plays a part in all types of abuse.

CONSEQUENCES OF EMOTIONAL ABUSE

When a child is refused the love and affection they crave they will begin to feel rejected, unloved and unsettled and these feeling can have a devastating affect on the child in later life.

They may show the following traits.

◆ Appear to try too hard to please other people in an attempt to feel accepted

◆ Be fearful of new people and situations

◆ Be unable to trust people

◆ Become anxious

◆ Become passive

◆ Become uncooperative and attention seeking, perhaps resorting to telling lies and becoming 'clingy' towards certain adults

◆ Develop speech impediments such as stuttering and stammering

◆ Find it difficult to accept praise

◆ Lack self-esteem

◆ May develop poor social skills and find it difficult to mix with other children of a similar age

◆ Regress with toilet training

◆ Resort to comfort-seeking behaviour such as thumb sucking or rocking

◆ Resort to deliberately hurting themselves – often seen as a 'cry for help'

◆ Resort to stealing

◆ Resort to tantrums due to frustration and a lack of acceptance

◆ Show aggression

◆ Suffer from an all round delay in their development

◆ Suffer from lack of concentration or lose interest in the things around them.

A FORM OF BULLYING

Emotional abuse is a form of bullying. Emotional abuse can be very difficult to spot as the signs or symptoms are rarely physical. Children who are subjected to emotional abuse are, therefore, very vulnerable. Emotional abuse in children can be suffered at the hands of adults, however it can also be in the form of bullying from other children. It is very serious and can have damaging long-term effects on the child.

UNINTENDED EMOTIONAL ABUSE

Sometimes adults can be guilty of emotional abuse without really meaning to and they may be absolutely horrified when they realise the effect their behaviour has on the child. For example, a child who is being pushed around at school by their peers may be told to 'stand up for themselves' or 'fight back' by a well meaning parent who may not fully understand the nature of the situation. Although the parent may only be trying to get the child to deal with the situation themselves, there is a real risk that the child will feel rejected, unworthy and useless. The child may then become anxious, frightened and nervous and by not being able to confide their feelings in their parents for fear of being told to 'grow up' they will become withdrawn. Although this is not intentional on the part of the parent, it is still a form of emotional abuse. Any child who seeks help from an adult, no matter how trivial the situation may appear, should be listened to and have their worries and concerns taken seriously.

UNREALISTIC EXPECTATIONS

Another form of emotional abuse, which can often be made with the child's best interests at heart, but which can in fact lead to feelings of inadequacy and disappointment, is when adults have unrealistic expectations of a child's abilities. It is a very common scenario and one which I am sure we have all been guilty of at some time: our child comes home from school having gained a very respectable grade in an examination and we hear ourselves asking how 'little Tommy did' or 'did Justine do better than you?'. As parents we want our children to be the top of the class and outshine our friends' children but is this really more important that encouraging our children to develop self-esteem and feel valued?

Likewise, a three-year-old who has just presented you with a painting will quickly become deflated when greeted with the words 'what is it?'. It is much better to invite the child to 'tell you about their picture' rather than admit you have no idea what it is supposed to be when they may have painstakingly spent two hours painting what they think is a work of art! All their hard work can be completely undone in a few seconds of thoughtlessness on the parent's behalf. Although these types of situations are far less serious than the emotional abuse suffered by children at the hands of uncaring, unloving adults and bullies, it should not be forgotten that a child's self-esteem and confidence can take a blow if not dealt with carefully and sensitively. It is absolutely vital that parents do not have unrealistic expectations of their child's abilities.

ADULTS WHO EMOTIONALLY ABUSE CHILDREN

Although we have looked at the signs and behavioural indicators of emotional abuse in a *child* already in this chapter, it is also important to be aware of the indications in an *adult* who may be an emotional abuser so that you can protect your child as much as possible.

Adults who emotionally abuse children may exhibit the following traits.

◆ Show an intense dislike to the child being abused

◆ Reject the child

◆ Be suffering from a mental illness

◆ Be a drug user

◆ Be a heavy drinker of alcohol

◆ Be volatile and unpredictable

◆ Have unreasonable expectations of the child with regard to both behaviour and academic success

◆ Have little or no understanding of how to command respect from others

◆ Have little or no understanding of how to manage a child's behaviour or how to discipline children effectively.

HOW TO PROTECT YOUR CHILD FROM EMOTIONAL ABUSE

As I have already mentioned earlier in this chapter, recognizing emotional abuse is not easy as there are often no *physical* signs. However you should be tuned into your own child and be aware of their usual behaviour. If they appear to show signs which are not consistent with their usual attitude then you should take notice and be vigilant. If your child tells you that someone is being unkind to them or if they show signs of anxiousness, become troublesome or indeed voice concerns to you then you should take these symptoms seriously. Once again, children who spend time in day care should also be watched closely for signs of attention-seeking behaviour or tantrums over and above the child's usual nature.

Of course, not all children are confident and outgoing by nature and this does not mean that all children who lack certain social skills or have little confidence are being emotionally abused. It simply means that there may be cause for concern if a child who is usually confident and outgoing suddenly becomes withdrawn and shy. If there are no reasonable explanations for a sudden change in your child's usual behaviour then you may need to look closer at their everyday situation and start to ask questions. Older children may show *physical* signs of emotional abuse and, of course, these are much easier to detect than the emotional suffering. For example, their weight may fluctuate dramatically as eating habits and dieting are often caused by very low self-esteem. The development of sudden speech disorders are also a sign of distress and poor self-image and many children and adolescents resort to deliberately hurting themselves as a form of gaining attention.

10

SEXUAL ABUSE

WHAT IS SEXUAL ABUSE?

Sexual abuse of children is when an adult uses the child for their own sexual gratification. Sexual abuse can take on many forms from exposing children to pornographic material to rape and it is extremely distressing and damaging to the child.

Sexual abuse can begin gradually and develop over a period of time and research suggests that, in most cases, it is carried out by an adult who is known to the child including relatives, family friends or people in a position of trust. This kind of abuse is extremely traumatic for the child and the adult abuser usually takes advantage of the child's innocence, trust and affection. Children are often threatened or bribed into remaining silent about the abuse they are suffering and the betrayal they experience leads to guilt and the feelings that the abuse they are suffering is their own fault. Sexual abuse can lead to long term emotional and physical damage and although the psychological effects may not be immediately apparent the child may find themselves unable to form loving, close and trusting relationships in later life.

Both boys and girls can be victims of sexual abuse although the majority of victims are female.

Forms of sexual abuse

Sexual abuse can take on many forms including:

- Being exposed to sexually explicit photographs, videos or webcams.

- Encouraging a child to take part in any form of sexual activity including stripping or masturbation.

- Failure to take adequate measures to prevent a child from being exposed to sexual activity by others.

- Genital or oral stimulation.

- Indecent exposure.

- Meeting a child following sexual 'grooming' with the intention of carrying out abuse.

- Rape.

- Sexual fondling of any part of the body, either clothed or unclothed, including using an object.

- Sexual intercourse.

- Taking, making or permitting to take, distributing, showing or advertising indecent images of children.

It is not always easy to know when a child is being sexually abused particularly if they deliberately try to hide the fact. Children are often very confused when suffering at the hands of an abuser in this way and they may be threatened by the abuser into keeping the abuse a secret. A child may not always realize that what they are suffering is abuse and they may even have been convinced by their abuser that what is happening is normal in families.

SIGNS OF SEXUAL ABUSE

There are some signs of sexual abuse that all parents should be aware of and act upon and these can be both physical and behavioural.

Physical signs

Physical signs of sexual abuse are the following.

◆ Bloodstains in underwear

◆ Difficulty in going to the toilet and showing distress when needing to pass urine or have a bowel movement

◆ Difficulty sitting down or walking/running

◆ Frequent 'accidents' when the child wets or soils themselves

◆ Frequent infections of the genital areas

◆ Non accidental bruising or scratching particularly around the genital areas

◆ Vaginal discharge.

Emotional and behavioural signs

Emotional and behavioural signs of sexual abuse are the following.

◆ Appearing depressed or withdrawn

◆ Avoiding being alone with certain people

◆ Dropping hints or clues to try to tell you what is happening to them – this is known as a covert disclosure

◆ Exposing the genital area

◆ Losing interest in school and starting to perform badly in school work

◆ Masturbating in public

◆ Painting or drawing images of a sexual nature

◆ Resorting to immature comfort behaviour such as rocking or thumb sucking not usually associated with a child of that age

◆ Showing insecurity

- Showing unexpected fear of certain people

- Undressing themselves at inappropriate times

- Using imaginary play to act out behaviour of a sexual nature

- Using sexual behaviour not usually associated with a child of that age

- Using sexual language not usually associated with a child of that age.

Of course not all of the above signs point to a child being abused and in many cases there may be a perfectly acceptable explanation. What is important however, is that if you are in any doubt you should not ignore the circumstances. Talk to your child and, if necessary seek guidance.

HOW TO PROTECT YOUR CHILD FROM SEXUAL ABUSE

It is impossible to describe a typical sex offender or paedophile. They do not look different from other people and they can often be found in all areas of society and from any professional, racial or religious background. It is often most shocking to learn that people in positions of trust, such as teachers, vicars etc., can be guilty of sexual abuse and, of course, in some circumstances, children suffer at the hands of their own parents, relatives or family friends. Many abusers feel they are doing no harm to the child and, contrary to popular belief, they often appear kind and concerned towards their victims. This is how they build on the relationship and gain the child's trust before then going on to abuse their victim without arousing suspicion or discovery.

Bearing this in mind therefore it can be very difficult to prevent or indeed detect sexual abuse, particularly if the child in question has been led to believe that the abuse is widely acceptable or is a result of their own actions.

Teaching your child about unacceptable behaviour

By helping your child to understand about sex and to learn about their own body you can encourage them to understand what is and is not acceptable behaviour. Some parents may feel uncomfortable about speaking to their child in this way but it can play an important part in protecting your child against abuse. Obviously how you approach the subject will be very much dependent on the age and level of understanding of your child but, once they have started to attend school, most children pick up on sexual information quickly from their peers, although this is often misunderstood and inaccurate.

If a child feels able to approach their parents in order to have things clarified and explained, it can help them enormously when understanding what is and is not acceptable behaviour. You will need to use your own common sense as to when to talk to your child about sexual matters. If your child has the courage to ask you a question about sex then return the compliment and treat their enquiry seriously. Never dismiss them or tell them they are too young to know. Children need to know that they can turn to their parents for help and advice if they are to refrain from turning to other, maybe less desirable, individuals for the information they crave.

◆ TIP ◆

Always answer your child's questions honestly. Never laugh at or ridicule your child's innocence. The more age appropriate information your child is armed with the more understanding they will have of what is and is not acceptable behaviour and they will be able to tell instinctively if what someone is doing to them is wrong.

CHECKLIST FOR PROTECTING YOUR CHILD AGAINST SEXUAL ABUSE

You can help your child to protect themselves against sexual abuse by:

✓ Answering their questions without ridicule

✓ Being honest and approachable

✓ Building an open and trusting relationship with your child

✓ Discouraging your child from keeping secrets

✓ Encouraging your child to learn about their own bodies

✓ Encouraging your child to tell you or another adult if something happens to them which they do not like or feel uncomfortable about

✓ Teaching your child that they have the right to say 'no' and to refuse anything they feel is wrong or which frightens them

11

NEGLECT

WHAT IS NEGLECT?

Neglect is when the parents or carers of a child do not provide them with adequate food, clothing, warmth, shelter, care and protection. A neglected child does not receive the appropriate care that they require in order to grow, develop and thrive, in other words they are left to fend for themselves. They may lack medical care and do not have their basic needs met. Parents who leave their children unattended may also be considered as having neglected them and this is a form of child abuse.

It is probably true to say that many parents who neglect their children do indeed love them, however they lack the fundamental knowledge of how to care for them adequately. The parents often have personal problems of their own which can also have a negative impact on the overall welfare of their child.

Signs of neglect

There are many signs and symptoms of neglect.

- The child may appear unkempt, dirty and smelly.

- The child may be underweight.

- The child may not have adequate clothing suitable for the time of year.

- The child may suffer frequent injuries due to lack of supervision.

- The child may suffer from minor infections and ailments on a regular basis which go untreated, such as earaches, coughs and toothache.

- The child may talk about being left alone or left to care for younger siblings.

- The child will appear to be hungry constantly.

- The child will be tired due to lack of sleep or irregular sleeping habits.

- The clothing the child does have may be dirty and unwashed and will often be ill fitting.

Parents and carers of neglected children are often very difficult to get hold of and even if an appointment is made, for example with the school, the parents will invariably fail to turn up.

LEAVING A CHILD HOME ALONE

Leaving a child at home alone can be classed as neglect. Although there is no legal age limit in Scotland, England and Wales at which a child can be left alone it is essential that parents think very carefully before leaving their child unattended. The law takes the view that a 13-year-old child can be very *mature* whereas a 15-year-old child can be equally *immature*. This is something that parents should take into account before deciding on how old their children should be before being left alone in the house. Despite the fact that there is no legal age limit, parents may be prosecuted for neglect if they leave a child alone in a manner which could be deemed unsafe or is likely to cause unnecessary suffering or injury to health.

The National Society for the Prevention of Cruelty to Children (NSPCC) advises that no child under the age of 12 should be left alone and that no-one under the age of 16 should be left alone overnight. Although many people may argue that this age is too high, it must be remembered that although some children appear capable of looking after themselves for short periods of time very few children aged between eight and 13 would be able to handle an emergency situation.

The NSPCC also advises that no-one under the age of 16 should be left to care for a baby. Parents should take this into account when arranging a babysitter or allowing their own child to babysit another.

HOW TO PROTECT YOUR CHILD FROM NEGLECT

Although most parents do not intentionally neglect their children it should be taken into account that there are many dangers in society today and it is the responsibility of the parents to ensure that these dangers are kept to a minimum. In short it is a parent's duty to minimise any potential risks to their child.

If you feel your child is old enough to start spending time on their own then you should ease them into the situation carefully and slowly. Build up the time they spend unsupervised and take into account some basic rules to ensure their safety, such as:

◆ Allow your child to have a friend to stay with them – preferably one they get on well with and someone who is trustworthy and mature minded.

◆ Eliminate any potential risks. Discourage children from carrying out any potentially dangerous tasks such as ironing or cooking. Ensure that smoke alarms are fitted and working properly. Don't leave older children in charge of younger ones.

◆ Explain safety procedures and leave adequate instructions in the event of an emergency.

◆ Explain to your child the dangers of answering the telephone or the door whilst they are alone.

◆ If you have a trustworthy, reliable neighbour whom you know well, inform them of your absence and ask them to keep an eye on your child. Likewise inform your child that the neighbour is available should they need anything.

♦ If you have *any* doubts whatsoever about leaving your child arrange for someone to stay with them.

♦ Leave contact numbers of trusted people and ensure that these people are contactable whilst you are away.

♦ Make sure that you are available to return if your child becomes distressed or is unhappy about anything.

♦ Make sure your child is aware of the dangers of being alone.

♦ Make sure your child is happy with the arrangement.

♦ Tell your child when you will be back.

12

LEARNING ABOUT PERSONAL SAFETY

Responsible parents can, and should, support their children in learning the basic requirements of how to keep themselves safe. Although accidents will happen to everyone at some point, it is necessary for children and young people to gain an understanding of how they can minimize any risks to themselves, how to avoid dangerous situations whenever possible, and how to deal with problems should they arise.

IMPORTANT POINTS TO REMEMBER

The important points for parents to remember are:

◆ Never wait until something bad happens *before* teaching your child about personal safety. This is a bit like 'locking the stable door after the horse has bolted' and will be of no benefit to your child at all. Preventing undesirable situations in the first place is the key and knowledge is crucial.

◆ Never use scare tactics in order to get your child's attention. Frightening your child into not wanting to be left alone or go out is not the answer as, of course, there will come a time when they will have to be alone and they will need the skills to deal with these everyday situations effectively.

◆ Never focus purely on a child you consider to be more 'at risk'. For example, if you have a son and a daughter you should not be of the opinion that only your daughter will be at risk of sexual abuse or that your son is more likely to be bullied. Neither should you concentrate solely on the safety of your disabled child if you have an able-bodied child as well.

♦ FACT ♦

Parents must remember that all children are vulnerable and, as such, they all need to be taught about personal safety.

CHANGING SITUATIONS

It is impossible for you as a parent to sit your child down one after-noon and give them a one or two hour lesson on how to keep safe. Personal safety is an ongoing subject which will change as your child gets older. It is something which you will need to tackle on a regular basis in order to ensure that your child has the skills and knowledge required to keep them safe in today's society.

As your child grows up and becomes more and more independent they will need more information about keeping safe. They will inevitably be spending more and more time away from the relative safety of their home environment and will no longer have their par-ents watching out for them. Your child will need you to help them to understand the dangers around them and to build on their confi-dence so that they will be equipped with the necessary knowledge to deal with frightening situations as and when they arise.

APPROACHING UNKNOWN ADULTS FOR HELP

One of the very sad consequences of the focus on 'stranger danger' in today's society is the lack of help and support which has invari-ably been lost. Although it is perfectly natural today for parents to tell their children not to speak to strangers the simple truth of the matter is *very few* strangers pose a threat to children on the streets today. Research proves that children are more at risk from people they know rather than strangers on the street. The focus on stranger danger has led many people, particularly men, to be wary of offering assistance to anyone showing distress purely because they are worried about being misunderstood. The result of this is that a child who appears to be lost on the streets or in a shopping arcade, may be ignored by passers by who are fearful of being accused of something sinister if they approach the child. As a parent it is therefore important that you talk to your child about such situations and think carefully about how you yourself would offer help to a young child who appears lost or distressed.

MANAGING INFORMATION

Newspapers, television and the use of the internet are all widely available and older children and teenagers are now very aware of the distress caused by the dangers on our streets. It is virtually impossible for parents to shield their children from the potential dangers on our streets and, shielding them is probably not advisable anyway. In order for children to know how to stay safe they need to know what they are up against without being frightened.

Newspapers and television regularly report about murders and missing children. The deaths of Sarah Payne in 2000, Holly Wells and Jessica Chapman in 2002 and more recently the abduction of Madeleine McCann from a holiday complex in Portugal in 2007 have all highlighted the very real dangers to our children. Distressing events such as these will invariably lead to questions and you may find yourself having a conversation with your child about such events. Always try to answer their questions honestly and openly but avoid scaring them. The very last thing you should be aiming for is to turn your child into a nervous wreck who is expecting someone to jump out on them from every street corner. Always try to deal with your child's questions as and when they arise without making too big an issue out of them. Dramatizing events and filling your child in on all the gory details is not advisable. Respond to their questions through ordinary conversations.

Often in the wake of a tragedy, such as in the case of the Soham murders when the community was devastated by the loss of two of their children, the children directly affected by this type of tragedy will be offered counselling. It is important to remember that most children, particularly those touched directly by tragedy, will prefer to talk to their own parents or most certainly to an adult they know and trust well rather than a stranger, however experienced and trained they may be in this kind of situation. A parent's love and understanding is often far more effective than counselling. Offering support to your child who may have lost a good friend through tragedy is never going to be easy and there is no right or wrong way to deal with this kind of situation. Listen to your child, let them tell you how they are feeling and give them time to grieve. Offer your support, answer their questions honestly and, most importantly, help them to keep things in perspective.

REASSURING YOUR CHILD

Parents will need to be honest with their children, no matter how hard this may be. There will be times when you may have to admit to your child that some adults are wicked and that they intention-ally want to harm children. Always back your comments up with reassurance by telling them that the majority of adults are good, kind and considerate people but there are some which they invari-ably need to be wary of.

BEING POLITE AND REMAINING SAFE

Encourage your child to practise certain rules which will take into account their own safety together with their rights.

♦ Never teach your child to be polite to *all* adults at *all* times. Encouraging your child to be polite and courteous should not be done in a way that makes your child accept that all adults are in control and that they have a right to demand politeness from them. If an adult behaves inappropriately towards a child it automatically removes any right to courteousness from the child.

◆ All too often we tell our children to 'do as they are told' and to obey the requests of adults. It is important that we teach our children that they do have a right to say 'no' and that if they are uncomfortable doing something they have been asked to do, they need to have the confidence to refuse the request.

◆ Often children are told not to 'answer back' when an adult tells them to do something and never to shout or raise their voice to an elder. However, if a child feels threatened or in danger then they should be encouraged to shout, scream and hit out if necessary.

Adults, parents included, need to understand that they cannot simply do as they please with children. Ground rules apply to everyone, children and adults alike. Parents need to help and encourage their children to make decisions and choices based on each situation. They need to gain the skills and confidence to weigh up the options and make the right decisions.

ENCOURAGING CHILDREN TO LEARN SAFE AND APPROPRIATE BEHAVIOUR

Your behaviour as a parent is absolutely crucial in encouraging your child to learn safe and appropriate behaviour. Dismissing their enquiries and not taking your child seriously will undermine their confidence and you will lose their respect and trust.

PERSONAL SAFETY CHECKLIST

Always:

✓ Listen to your child and help them to make decisions and choices. If they are struggling with a decision, listen to their concerns and worries, offer help and guidance whilst still allowing them to decide what to do.

✓ Show your child respect and trust in order to build on their confidence and self-esteem.

✓ Teach your child about boundaries and ground rules. Make sure that they understand that they have a right to say 'no' to something they are not happy about or which does not feel right.

✓ Encourage your child to learn about their body. Talk to them about who should touch them and the reasons for this. This is a good time to introduce other aspects of personal care such as doctors, dentists etc. It is a good way of building on a child's awareness of their body. Encourage your child to respect their own bodies and to have the confidence and knowledge to know what is right and wrong.

✓ Encourage your child to take responsibility for their own personal care and hygiene as soon as possible. This will help them to build on their confidence and self-esteem.

✓ Respect your child's privacy. Keeping your child safe and protecting them from danger is not an excuse to look through their diaries and text messages or to rifle through their belongings in the hope of finding clues to their whereabouts or friends.

✓ Avoid falling into the trap of telling children that 'strangers' are the main source of danger to children. This kind of information can be very misleading for them. Children are in fact more at risk from adults with whom they are already acquainted and these may be either well known, such as friends or family, or recognizable, such as a person living or working locally to them.

✓ Avoid encouraging children to believe that only adults are capable of causing them harm and distress. Help them to have the confidence to speak up about another child who may be bullying them either at home, school or in the local neighbourhood.

✓ Make sure that your child or teenager understands that, although the media focuses heavily on tragedy and child murders, these are very rare. Children who die young usually do so as the result of a road or domestic accident or illness rather than through abduction or murder. It can be very damaging to children to try to build everyday rules based on very rare tragic circumstances.

◆ **FACT** ◆

Adults are mainly responsible for protecting children. As a parent you should never give your child the impression that they are totally responsible for their own protection.

Children who have been encouraged to act sensibly and know how to avoid danger and, if faced with a frightening situation, have been given the correct skills to deal with it may still find themselves being abused. A child should *never* be made to feel that the abuse they have suffered is in any way their own fault. The abuser is the one at fault. This is *not* the fault of the child and they must never be made to feel as though they have failed.

13

DEALING WITH ACCIDENTS

The definition of the word 'accident' is an 'incident which happens unexpectedly'.

Although often avoidable, accidents can happen to anyone at anytime and even the most diligent of parents can not be expected to protect their child all of the time. However, it is how you respond to an accident which can make all the difference to the outcome.

This chapter will look at some of the more common accidents suffered by children, how to avoid them and how to treat them should they occur.

◆ IMPORTANT ◆

When dealing with any accident or emergency situation it is vital that you remain calm.

CHOKING

One of the most common 'accidents' suffered by babies and children is choking. Babies and young children usually explore objects using their mouths and it therefore goes without saying that you should take care not to allow small objects to come into their reach. Always make sure that children are sat down to eat and that babies are never left propped up with a bottle. Never give small children whole nuts, hard sweets or small fruits, such as whole grapes.

Signs of choking

If your child is choking they will:

♦ Have difficulty breathing

♦ Appear flushed in the face and neck

♦ Make strange noises or no sounds at all

♦ Their skin will begin to turn grey-blue

Initial treatment: back slaps

To treat a child who is choking follow these steps:

1. Bend the child forwards.

2. Give up to five sharp slaps between the shoulder blades with *one* hand.

3. Check inside the mouth and scoop out any *obvious* obstruction.

If choking persists, give up to five more back slaps and, one again, check the mouth for any obvious obstruction.

♦ **IMPORTANT** ♦

Never put your fingers in the mouth or blindly down the throat to try to dislodge an obstruction. Always scoop the object out with one finger.

Subsequent treatment: chest thrusts

If the back slaps fail then:

1. Stand or kneel behind the child.

2. Make a fist and place this below the child's lower breastbone.

3. Grasp this fist with your other hand and press into the chest with a sharp inward thrust up to five times at a rate of one every three seconds.

4. Check the mouth again for any *obvious* obstruction.

If the choking persists give up to five more back slaps and, once again, check the mouth for any obvious obstruction.

Subsequent treatment: abdominal thrusts
If this still does not dislodge the obstruction then give up to five abdominal thrusts as described below:

1. Make a fist and place it against the child's central upper abdomen.

2. Grasp your fist with your other hand and press with a sharp upward thrust up to five times.

3. Check the mouth for any *obvious* obstruction.

If none of these work you *must* call for medical assistance. Dial 999 and continue repeating the cycle of back slaps and chest and abdominal thrusts until the ambulance arrives.

Treating a baby for choking
If your baby is choking you will need to follow a different routine as abdominal thrusts could seriously injure their internal organs.

Initial treatment: back slaps
To administer back slaps to a baby follow these steps:

1. Lay the baby face down along your forearm.

2. Keep the baby's head low.

3. Give up to five sharp slaps on the back.

4. Turn the baby face up on your lap and remove any *obvious* obstruction.

Subsequent treatment: chest thrusts
If the back slaps fail to dislodge the obstruction and the baby continues to choke then give up to five chest thrusts following these steps:

1. Place two fingers on the lower half of the baby's breastbone, one finger's breadth below the nipple line.

2. Give up to five sharp thrusts into the chest.

3. Check the baby's mouth for any *obvious* obstruction.

Repeat the back slaps and chest thrusts three times. If the obstruction has not cleared then you *must* call for assistance. Do not leave the baby unattended, take him or her with you to the telephone and dial 999. Continue to administer back slaps and chest thrusts as described above until the ambulance arrives.

BLEEDING

The sight of blood often reduces most people to a nervous wreck and puts them into a blind panic. Children are no exception. An injury which causes little pain can bring about hysteria if blood is spotted! It is very important that you keep calm in order to reassure your child and that you act quickly particularly if the wound is bleeding severely.

Minor wounds

For minor wounds or cuts:

1. Wash the area with clean tap water.

2. Apply a plaster or dry bandage.

Serious wounds

For serious wounds or cuts follow this procedure.

1. Remove or cut the clothing to expose the wound.

2. If you have a sterile dressing or pad immediately to hand then cover the wound, if not apply direct pressure over the wound with your fingers or the palm of your hand.

3. If there is something embedded in the wound *do not remove it*. Apply pressure to either side of the wound.

4. Raise the injured body part above the casualty's heart.

5. Lay the casualty down.

6. Apply a sterile dressing over the original pad you may have used – do not remove the original pad – and bandage firmly in place.

7. If the blood seeps through the first bandage do not remove it, bandage another pad on top.

8. Call 999 for an ambulance.

9. Whilst waiting for medical assistance to arrive, check the casualty's circulation and, if necessary, slightly loosen the bandage.

10. Keep an eye on the casualty's appearance and monitor and record their breathing, pulse and level of response.

Nose bleeds

For nose bleeds following this procedure.

1. Sit the child down with their head bent forwards.

2. Pinch the soft part of the nose between your thumb and index finger until the bleeding stops.

3. If the nose is still bleeding after 20 minutes, telephone your GP for advice.

ACCIDENTAL POISONING

Young children can easily mistake medicines and chemicals for sweets and drinks. It is paramount that you ensure that you store all medicines, cleaning equipment, makeup etc. in their original containers and out of the reach of young children to avoid accidental poisoning.

◆ **IMPORTANT** ◆

If you suspect that your child has swallowed any poisonous substance *do not* attempt to induce vomiting.

Follow this procedure if your child has swallowed something harmful.

1. If there is vomit in the child's mouth, lay them on their side to allow it to drain away.

2. If the child stops breathing you will need to carry out mouth to mouth ventilation as described in Chapter 15.

3. Call an ambulance immediately and give as much information as possible about the poison the child has swallowed.

4. Whilst waiting for the ambulance to arrive, monitor and record their breathing, pulse and level of response every ten minutes.

5. If the child is conscious and has suffered from burnt lips as a result of swallowing the poison then offer frequent sips of cold water or milk.

◆ **IMPORTANT** ◆

Take the container of poison with you to the hospital so that the medical staff can see exactly what the child has swallowed.

BURNS OR SCALDS

Babies and young children are inquisitive. It is up to you as a parent to ensure that the environment they have access to is safe and free from any risk. However, the home contains many potential hazards which may pose a threat from burns.

These include:

◆ Fires

◆ Hot drinks

◆ Kettles

◆ Irons

◆ Candles

◆ Bath water

◆ Pans.

Reducing the risk of burns

In the majority of cases, accidents from burns can be avoided.

◆ Always make sure that children cannot get access to the kitchen unsupervised.

◆ Never allow young children near hot objects or liquids.

◆ Place the kettle far back on the kitchen work surface.

◆ Make sure there are no flexes hanging over the edge.

◆ Turn pan handles away from the edge of the cooker.

◆ Always use a fireguard.

Never underestimate the sun's rays and remember that babies and young children can develop serious burns from the sun if they are not adequately protected.

Treatment of burns or scalds

If your child has suffered from a burn or scald, follow these steps:-

1. Make the child comfortable.

2. Pour cold water on the burn for ten minutes. If the burn is of a chemical nature increase this time to at least 20 minutes.

3. When cooling the burn with water, keep an eye on your child for signs of breathing difficulties and, if necessary, be prepared to resuscitate – see Chapter 15.

4. Remove any clothing or jewellery from around the affected area as the injury will begin to swell up and rings, necklaces, bracelets, shoes or tight clothing may restrict the flow of blood.

5. Cover the burn and the surrounding area with a sterile dressing or a clean piece of non-fluffy material such as a cotton handkerchief or tea towel. If the burn is to the child's face do not cover it, but keep on cooling the area with water until help arrives.

6. Take your child to the hospital or telephone for an ambulance.

◆ **IMPORTANT** ◆

Do not burst any blisters or apply any creams, lotions, ointments or fat to a burn. Avoid touching the affected area.

FALLS

Young children are very prone to falls. Most children rush around, falling over and banging into things and usually these everyday falls are not a problem.

Treatment of falls

If your child has a bad fall you should follow these steps:

1. Reassure your child and, if they are old enough, get them to tell you where they are hurting.

2. If your child appears to have injured their back or their neck it is vital that you *do not move them*. Telephone for an ambulance immediately.

3. If your child is unconscious, but you are certain that they have not suffered from an injury to their back or neck then place them in the recovery position (see Chapter 15) and telephone for an ambulance immediately.

4. Take your child to the hospital if they have difficulty moving any part of their body or they are in pain as this could indicate a broken bone.

5. Take your child to the hospital if they are dazed, are vomiting or if they have difficulty focusing or hearing.

Reducing the risk of falls

You can reduce the risk of falls by providing constant supervision for your baby and young child, fitting safety catches to windows and tidying toys away to ensure that your floor space is as clutter free as possible. Make sure that you use stair gates and teach your child how to use the stairs correctly.

DROWNING

It is possible for small children to drown in only a few centimetres of water. *Never* allow your child to play in or near to water unsupervised and teach them to swim as soon as possible.

If your child is drowning follow these steps:

1. Remove them from the water.

2. Dial 999 immediately and ask for an ambulance.

3. If your child has stopped breathing you will need to carry out mouth to mouth ventilation as described in Chapter 15.

4. If your child is breathing then put them in the recovery position as described in Chapter 15 and monitor their progress until help arrives.

How you respond to an accident could make all the difference. Stay calm, assess the situation and treat the casualty accordingly. If possible, enrol on a basic first aid course to give you the necessary information needed to deal with everyday accidents.

14

DEALING WITH COMMON ILLNESSES

All children will become ill from time to time and often the illness will not be serious or cause too much concern. However, occasionally a high temperature or a rash can be the warning signs of something severe which may need immediate hospital treatment.

Media attention has highlighted the risk of meningitis and most parents are now aware of the immediate need to get their child to the hospital should they suspect this illness. However not all parents are adept at spotting the warning signs. This chapter will look at some of the more common illnesses in children, how to spot them and how to treat them.

ALLERGIC REACTIONS

Symptoms of allergic reactions

People can be allergic to many things. The main symptoms of an allergic reaction are:

◆ Red, blotchy or itchy skin

◆ Anxiety

◆ Swelling of the face and neck

◆ Puffy eyes

◆ Breathing problems

◆ Rapid pulse.

Although most allergic reactions are not serious and will simply result in a little discomfort, others such as nut allergies or bee stings can be very serious and result in anaphylactic shock. This means that breathing becomes difficult, and as the airways swell up it is often impossible to breathe. Children can die from anaphylactic shock so it is vital that medical assistance is sought immediately.

◆ **IMPORTANT** ◆

If your child has severe allergic reactions make sure that everyone who may be caring for them is aware of the situation and that they know what to avoid and how to deal with a reaction if necessary.

ASTHMA ATTACKS

◆ **IMPORTANT** ◆

If your child suffers from asthma make sure that they know how to use their inhaler as prescribed and that you never run out of medication.

Symptoms of an asthma attack

Asthma is very common in children. The main signs of an asthma attack are:

◆ Difficulty in breathing

◆ Wheezing

◆ Difficulty in speaking

◆ Dry, tickly cough

◆ A grey/blue tinge to the skin.

Treating an asthma attack

It is very important that the sufferer is kept calm. Talk to them and reassure them. Make them comfortable by sitting them up, leaning slightly forward, to make breathing easier. *Never* lay the casualty down. Help the casualty to find their inhaler. They need to take their *reliever* inhaler which is usually blue and not the *preventer* inhaler. The inhaler should take effect within minutes. If the attack begins to ease over the next 5 to 10 minutes then get the casualty to take another dose from the inhaler and encourage them to breathe slowly and deeply. Inform the doctor if this is their first attack or if the attack is severe.

◆ IMPORTANT ◆

If the reliever inhaler has no effect after 5 to 10 minutes then you must call an ambulance. Get the casualty to keep using the reliever inhaler every 5 to 10 minutes. Monitor and record their breathing and pulse every ten minutes whilst waiting for the ambulance to arrive. If the casualty falls unconscious then you must be prepared to resuscitate if necessary as described in Chapter 15.

FEBRILE CONVULSIONS

Febrile convulsions are fits or seizures which sometimes occur when a child has a high temperature, usually over 39°C (102°F). These fits or seizures will usually occur between the ages of six months and six years and they can be quite frightening for parents who often mistake them for epileptic fits. Epilepsy is however, not caused by a high temperature. A child who has one febrile convulsion is more likely to go on to have another.

Most febrile convulsions last less than five minutes. If your child's seizure goes on for more than this length of time you should call for an ambulance.

Symptoms of febrile convulsions

Common symptoms of febrile convulsions are:

◆ The child will appear hot and flushed due to their high temperature.

◆ They will be dazed and confused.

- They may lose consciousness – be prepared for this and make sure that they are not standing up.

- Their muscles will tighten.

- They may moan or cry out.

- They could stop breathing for up to 30 seconds.

- Their skin may turn blue.

- The muscles in the arms, legs, face and other parts of the body will twitch and shake.

- The eyes may roll backwards.

- They may lose control of their bowels or bladder.

Although a febrile convulsion can be quite alarming they are usually short lived and the child will usually make a full recovery.

Treating a febrile convulsions

To treat a child who is suffering from a febrile convulsion follow these steps.

1. Remove any excess clothing to cool the child down.

2. Protect the child from any injury – remove any nearby objects and surround the child with cushions.

3. Sponge the child's body with tepid water starting at the head and working down.

4. Put the child in the recovery position making sure the head is tilted well back to avoid choking on the tongue or vomit.

5. Call for an ambulance.

◆ IMPORTANT ◆

Never use force to restrain a child who is experiencing a febrile convulsion. Remove nearby objects to avoid injury.

DIARRHOEA AND VOMITING

Diarrhoea and vomiting are not unusual in children and can often be treated successfully at home. However, if your child shows other signs of illness or does not respond to the treatment you have administered then you should seek medical advice immediately.

Treating diarrhoea and vomiting

If your child is suffering from diarrhoea and or vomiting follow these guidelines:

◆ Babies which are breastfed should continue to be fed as normal.

◆ Babies who are bottle fed should be given small quantities of rehydration fluids, which can be purchased from the chemist, and have their milk reintroduced gradually.

◆ Older children can be given sips of rehydration fluid initially. Gradually increase their liquid intake but avoid offering milk for at least 24 hours.

◆ After approximately 8 to 10 hours, reintroduce food by offering very bland foods such as toast. Do not offer your child fatty or spicy foods as this will just aggravate the problem.

◆ IMPORTANT ◆

If your child has been suffering from diarrhoea or vomiting for more than 24 hours, has a high temperature or has blood in their diarrhoea or vomit you must seek medical assistance immediately.

Reducing the risk of diarrhoea and vomiting

Although diarrhoea and vomiting is common in children, largely due to their lack of hygiene skills, there are ways of reducing the risk of this illness.

◆ Encourage your child to practise good hygiene methods and teach them how to wash their hands effectively. There is more on effective hand-washing routines in Chapter 1.

◆ Make sure that *you* practise good hygiene methods and wash your hands after using the toilet and before preparing foods or formula milk.

◆ Make sure that you store food correctly and that any food which is past its use by date is thrown away.

◆ Cook food thoroughly.

◆ Keep your kitchen surfaces clean.

◆ Handle and store cooked and raw foods carefully.

◆ Clean up thoroughly after someone has been ill.

There is more about preventative measures in Chapter 1.

HIGH TEMPERATURE

There are many reasons why a child's temperature may rise. They could be feeling unwell or coming down with a common illness such as a cold or other virus, or it may be a sign of something more serious. A raised temperature indicates that the body is fighting an infection.

Taking your child's temperature
To take your child's temperature do the following.

Babies – Place the thermometer under your baby's arm and leave in place for three minutes.
Children – Place the thermometer under your child's tongue and leave in place for three minutes.

Bringing a temperature down
Normal body temperature is 37°C (98.6°F). If your child's temperature rises above 38°C (100.4°F) and they feel flushed and appear sweaty, then you will need to bring their temperature down.

You can do this by following these steps:

◆ Make sure the room is not too hot. The ideal room temperature should be about 15°C or 60°F.

- ◆ Remove excess clothing. If necessary, strip your child down to their underwear.

- ◆ If your child is in bed, use a light sheet rather than a duvet or blanket.

- ◆ Sponge your child with lukewarm water paying particular attention to their hands, face and upper body.

- ◆ Give your child plenty of fluids. Drinks of cool water are ideal.

◆ IMPORTANT ◆

Bring down a high temperature to avoid your child being at risk from convulsions.

MENINGITIS

Meningococcal bacteria can cause meningitis and septicaemia (blood poisoning). They often occur together. Meningitis is an inflammation of the lining surrounding the brain and spinal cord. Those most at risk are babies, young children, teenagers and young adults.

It is not always easy to spot the signs of meningitis and septicaemia and, in the early stages, the symptoms can resemble those of flu. It is vital that you know the difference and are able to recognize the signs, as early diagnosis can mean the difference between life and death.

It is impossible to know when meningitis or septicaemia will strike or who it will affect. The most common form of permanent damage is deafness. In severe cases, where septicaemia has occurred, it may be necessary for fingers, toes or even limbs to be amputated.

Symptoms of meningitis and septicaemia

Babies and toddlers
Common symptoms of meningitis and septicaemia in babies and toddlers include:

- Fever – coupled with cold hands and feet
- Refusal of food
- Vomiting
- Fretful, dislike of being handled
- Pale, blotchy skin
- Blank, staring expression
- Drowsy – may be difficult to wake
- Stiff neck
- Arched back
- High-pitched cry.

Children and adults

Common symptoms of meningitis and septicaemia in children and adults include:

- Fever – coupled with cold hands and feet
- Vomiting
- Headache
- Stiff neck
- Dislike of bright lights
- Joint/muscle pain
- Drowsy – may be difficult to wake
- Confusion.

Much has been reported about the rash which is sometimes present with meningitis. The rash does not fade under pressure when you carry out the 'glass test'.

Glass test – Press the side of a clear glass firmly against the skin. If the rash disappears, it is not meningitis. If it remains, call an ambulance immediately.

◆ **IMPORTANT** ◆

A rash is not always present in the case of meningitis and septicaemia and it is important that you take into account all of the potential symptoms and not simply look for a rash.

Other symptoms of meningitis and septicaemia may include rapid breathing, stomach cramps and diarrhoea. If you suspect that your child has meningitis or septicaemia it is absolutely vital that you call for medical assistance immediately.

◆ **FACT** ◆

Septicaemia is a medical emergency. You can help to reduce the risk of contracting two types of meningitis by making sure that your child is given the Hib and Meningococcus C vaccinations. However, it is important to remember that vaccinations are not yet available for all forms of meningitis. Parents must remain alert even if their children have been vaccinated.

MEASLES

Measles is a highly infectious viral disease that causes a range of symptoms which include a fever and distinctive red-brown spots. The rash itself is the most well known and obvious sign of measles however, it is actually just an outward symptom of what is mainly a respiratory infection.

Measles mainly affects young children but it can be caught at any age. The virus can be spread by droplets in the air carried by coughs and sneezes, contact with the skin or via objects carrying the live virus.

Thanks to the MMR vaccination (Mumps, Measles and Rubella), measles has become something of a rarity in the United Kingdom, however there have been recent outbreaks in children who have not been immunized.

Common symptoms of measles

Approximately 9 to 11 days after becoming infected, your child may experience the following symptoms:

◆ Cold-like symptoms such as a runny nose, sneezing and watery eyes.

◆ Red, swollen eyes which are sensitive to light.

◆ A temperature which may last for several days.

◆ Fatigue

◆ Irritability

◆ Aches and pains

◆ Loss of appetite

◆ Dry cough

◆ Red-brown spots which will usually appear 3 to 4 days after the first symptoms and last for up to 8 days. The spots will usually start behind the ears, spread around the head and neck and develop onto the legs and the rest of the body. The spots usually start small but they will quickly increase in size and join together.

Treating measles

It is often quite easy to treat measles and usually reducing the fever and allowing plenty of rest is all that is needed for a full recovery. Providing there are no complications, the patient will usually make a full recovery within 7 to 10 days.

Follow these steps to treat measles effectively:

◆ Monitor your child's temperature.

◆ Keep their temperature down as much as possible, but do not allow your child to become cold.

◆ Liquid paracetamol can be given to ease aches and pains and to reduce fever. Do not give aspirin to children under the age of 16 years.

- If your child's eyes are sensitive to light, try dimming lights or closing curtains to ease their sensitivity.

- Make the room humid by placing a bowl of water in the room. This should help to relieve any cough as cough medicines are of little help.

- Do not allow your child to become dehydrated. Small children lose water rapidly which will make any cough they may have even worse.

Antibiotics are of no use when treating measles as the disease is viral; however they may be prescribed for any secondary bacterial infections.

Although measles, without any complications, can be treated effectively without medical treatment, you should consult your doctor if you suspect your child has contracted them and have the symptoms confirmed.

It is important also that you seek medical advice if:

- the symptoms worsen

- your child's temperature exceeds 38°C

- their temperature remains high after the other symptoms have ceased

- there are any other signs of illness.

CHICKENPOX

Chickenpox is caused by the virus Herpes Zoster. It is a mild disease which most children will catch at sometime during their childhood though it is most common between the ages of two and eight. Winter and Spring are the times of year when the infection seems most common. Usually lots of children are affected at the same time, around once every three years, bringing about an epidemic.

The patient is infectious from around two days before the rash appears until approximately five days afterwards. The incubation period, the time from coming in contact with the virus to showing symptoms of the disease, is between 10 and 21 days. Chickenpox is spread in tiny droplets of saliva and nasal mucus coughed out by an infected person and, because the virus is already present in these droplets prior to any rash appearing, the virus spreads quickly.

The chickenpox rash is made up of lots of blisters which burst and then scab over. The Health Protection Agency recommends that children can begin to mix with other children in school, nursery, childcare settings etc. once the blisters have fully scabbed over and this process usually takes approximately 5 to 7 days after the first scab has appeared. Once the last blister has burst and scabbed over, it can be safely assumed that the child is no longer infectious.

 **REMEMBER** ◆

Chickenpox is a mild disease which rarely needs medical treatment. Apply calamine lotion to soothe the itching.

Shingles

After the chickenpox infection, the Herpes Zoster virus remains dormant in the body's nerve tissues. The body's immune system keeps the virus under control, however the virus can be reactivated at a later time in life, usually during adulthood, causing shingles. The cause for shingles is unknown although it is associated with a weak immune system perhaps due to having treatment for cancer or because the body is getting older. The first sign of shingles is usually a pain in the area of the affected nerve. Approximately seven days later a rash will usually appear, followed by blisters which tend to only affect one side of the body.

EAR INFECTIONS

Ear infections are quite common in young children and they occur when bacteria or viruses cause swelling and irritation in the ear. Although ear infections can be very uncomfortable they are rarely serious. Fluid, which builds up behind the eardrum can cause a lot of pressure on the membrane causing a hole to form and this is known as a perforated eardrum. In most cases these will heal by themselves. Very occasionally complications can arise from an ear infection and lead to meningitis. Most ear infections however are unlikely to cause permanent loss or impairment of hearing. If your child's infections keep reoccurring it may be worth talking to your GP who may refer your child to an Ear, Nose and Throat specialist for further treatment. This could be in the form of the insertion of tiny tubes to help drain fluid, known as grommets.

Symptoms of an ear infection

The symptoms of an ear infection are usually, swelling, itching and discomfort. If the middle ear becomes infected your child may experience pain, a high temperature, slight deafness, tiredness and nausea. You may notice a fluid or yellow/green pus coming out of the ear.

Treating an ear infection

In most cases an ear infection will clear up without medical treatment in around three days. Your pharmacist may be able to recommend over-the-counter treatments, such as drops, to reduce the swelling and ease any pressure building up in the ear.

If your child has a lot of pain or you are worried about their ear infection you must contact your doctor. If the infection turns out to be a bacterial one then it will need to be treated with antibiotics. It is not always easy for doctors to tell the difference between a viral or bacterial infection and although antibiotics are very effective against bacterial infections they will not work on viral ones.

Keeping your child healthy and free from illness is all part of keeping them safe. Although childhood illnesses are very common it is important that parents do not overestimate their own medical knowledge. If you are in any doubt whatsoever, if your child's health deteriorates or you are worried about their state of health in any way it is vital that you seek medical advice immediately.

15

BASIC FIRST AID

All children will suffer from accidents from time to time, some more serious than others. Your child will also, inevitably, succumb to illness at some point during their childhood and it is absolutely vital that all parents have some knowledge of first aid in order to deal with these situations.

Whilst it is essential that parents are equipped with the necessary knowledge for them to deal successfully with an accident or emergency we should also know our limitations. If you are in any doubt whatsoever, you should seek professional advice. Often, the very first steps taken in the event of an accident can have a lasting outcome on the child's recovery and all parents should be knowledgeable on how to deal with everyday common illnesses and accidents.

This chapter will give help and advice on how to administer basic first aid, however, it is important that medical assistance is also sought.

FIRST AID KIT

A well stocked first aid kit, kept out of reach of children but within easy reach of adults, is a necessity in every home. Gathering together emergency supplies in a medical box and quickly replacing any of the items you have used will help you to handle an emergency situation easily and effectively. Choose a light-weight, durable and easy-to-carry container to hold your first aid equipment and make sure that everyone knows where the equipment is kept. If your children are old enough to understand, explain to them how to use the first aid box contents in an emergency and review the first aid manual with them.

Contents of a first aid kit

You should be able to deal with everyday accidents by equipping your medical kit with the following items:

- A first aid manual
- A thermometer
- Adhesive tape
- An eye bath
- A bottle of eye wash
- Antiseptic wipes
- Dressings in assorted sizes
- Elastoplasts in assorted sizes
- Paracetamol syrups for children
- Rehydration solutions
- Several pairs of disposable gloves
- Sharp scissors
- Sterile gauze
- Triangular bandages
- Tweezers.

THE PRELIMINARY STAGES OF FIRST AID

Before we look at the types of ailments a child can suffer from it is important that parents are aware of the preliminary stages which can be vital to the outcome.

These stages include:

◆ Assessing the situation

◆ Assessing the casualty

◆ Breathing for the casualty

◆ Cardio-pulmonary Resuscitation (CPR)

◆ The recovery position.

Assessing the situation

All accidents should be approached with caution. The overwhelming desire for a parent to go rushing in to assist their child is very common. It is vital that you stop, think and assess the situation you are faced with before ploughing straight in. Putting yourself and other members of your family in danger will do absolutely nothing to help your injured child but may well prove disastrous for them if what you do in the first few seconds is rash and inappropriate.

Your own safety is paramount if you are to assist anyone else and this should be at the forefront of your thoughts at all times. No-one is doubting that you will have a sudden urge to rush to your injured child, scoop them up and try to tend their injuries but, as I have already said, this can have devastating effects if you do not assess the situation first. A child with a neck injury, for example, may suffer irreparable damage if they are moved in this way.

Follow these simple steps in order to successfully assess the situation *before* taking any action.

Ask yourself:

◆ Are there any risks to yourself or the casualty? If there are, put your own safety first in order to assist the casualty. If possible, remove the danger from the casualty. If this is not possible, remove the casualty from the danger.

Assessing the casualty

When the situation is safe, ask yourself:

◆ Is the casualty visibly conscious? If they have collapsed, try shaking them gently by the shoulders, and talking to them to see if they respond.

If they do respond, treat their injuries (more on this later in the chapter) and, if necessary, call for an ambulance. If you are at all unsure or if the casualty has suffered a head injury always get them checked out by the emergency services.

A non-responsive casualty

If the casualty does not respond when gently shaken and spoken to then you need to assess how the accident has happened and weigh up your options. If the condition is due to injury or drowning and you are not alone then ask the person you are with to call an ambulance immediately and pass on the details of the injured person.

If you are alone then it is vital that you do not waste any time. You will need to call an ambulance immediately and, if the casualty is not breathing you will need to carry out emergency resuscitation. If the casualty is a child you must carry out emergency resuscitation for **one minute** before calling an ambulance. If the casualty is not breathing you must respond by breathing for them using mouth to mouth resuscitation. Waiting for the emergency services to arrive will result in certain death. Your response at this time is crucial.

Breathing for the casualty

To carry out resuscitation you need to do the following.

1. Gently tilt the head of the casualty well back and check for signs of breathing. This can be done by looking for the chest movements and listening for sounds of breathing. Put your cheek close to the casualty's mouth and feel for their breath. Take up to ten seconds to check for breathing. If the casualty is breathing

then you need to place them in the recovery position whilst you wait for the ambulance to arrive (see page 155). If the casualty is not breathing then you will need to breathe for them.

2. Open the airway before administering any breaths. To do this, place two fingers under the casualty's chin and your other hand on their forehead and tilt the head well back. If the casualty is a baby, place only one finger under their chin. Remove any *obvious* obstruction from the mouth by swiftly scooping the object sideways with one finger. *Do not* delve into the mouth to try to remove objects which cannot easily be seen.

3. Use your thumb and index finger to pinch the casualty's nose firmly. It is vital that the nostrils are tightly closed to prevent air from escaping.

4. Take a full breath. Place your lips around the casualty's lips and make a good seal. If the casualty is a baby then place your lips tightly around the mouth *and* nose.

5. Blow into the mouth until the chest rises. It will take about two seconds for full inflation.

6. Keep your hands in the same position and remove your lips to allow the chest to fall fully.

7. Repeat the mouth to mouth procedure once more.

8. Check the pulse. To do this place two fingers on the carotid pulse in the casualty's neck. If there is no pulse then move onto CPR (see below). If a pulse is present continue with mouth to mouth ventilation until breathing returns or the emergency services arrive, whichever is the sooner. If breathing does return then place the casualty in the recovery position and keep checking their progress until the emergency services arrive.

CARDIO-PULMONARY RESUSCITATION (CPR)

If, after assessing the casualty, you cannot find a pulse or there are no other signs of recovery then you must begin Cardio-pulmonary Resuscitation (CPR) immediately.

CPR for adults and older children

If the casualty is a child of eight years old or over, or an adult, follow these steps:

1. Lay the casualty on their back and kneel beside them.

2. Place the middle finger of your lower hand over the point where the lowermost ribs meet the breastbone.

3. Place your index finger above it on the breastbone.

4. Place the heel of your other hand on the breastbone and slide it down to meet your index finger.

5. Place the heel of your first hand on top of the other hand and interlock your fingers.

6. Lean well over the casualty with your arms straight.

7. Press down vertically on the breastbone and depress by approximately 4 to 5 cms (1.5 to 2 inches)

8. Complete 15 chest compressions. You should be aiming for about a hundred per minute.

9. After 15 chest compressions give two breaths of mouth to mouth ventilation following the instructions given previously.

10. Continue alternating 15 chest compressions with two breaths of mouth to mouth ventilation.

CPR for young children

If the casualty is a child aged from 1 to 7 years follow these steps:

1. Position your hand as you would for an adult (see above). However, as the child is smaller use the heel of only *one* hand.

2. Press down sharply this time to a third of the depth of the chest.

3. Do this five times at a rate of 100 per minute.

4. Give one breath of mouth to mouth ventilation.

5. Alternate five chest compressions with one breath of mouth to mouth ventilation for one minute *before* calling an ambulance and continue with the compressions and breaths whilst waiting for the emergency services to arrive.

CPR for babies

If the casualty is a baby under the age of 12 months follow these steps:

1. Place the tips of two fingers one finger's breadth below the nipple line of the baby.

2. Press down sharply at this point to a third of the depth of the chest.

3. Do this five times at a rate of 100 per minute.

4. Give one breath of mouth to mouth ventilation.

5. Alternate five chest compressions with one breath of mouth to mouth ventilation for one minute *before* calling an ambulance and whilst waiting for the emergency services to arrive.

◆ **QUICK CHECK** ◆

Adults and children over eight years old
15 chest compressions at a rate of 100 per minute using two hands on the chest to two breaths of mouth to mouth ventilation.

Children aged 1 to 7
5 chest compressions at a rate of 100 per minute using one hand on the chest to one breath of mouth to mouth ventilation.

Babies under 12 months
5 chest compressions at a rate of 100 per minute using two fingers on the nipple line to one breath of mouth to mouth ventilation.

◆ **REMEMBER** ◆

The rule for chest compressions and mouth to mouth ventilation is:

'15–2 for someone like you' (adult or child over 8)

'5–1 for a little one' (baby or a child under 8)

THE RECOVERY POSITION

If the casualty is breathing you should place them in the recovery position whilst you are waiting for the emergency services to arrive. The following steps take you through the recovery position, however, if you suspect a back or neck injury then the position should be modified as stated.

1. Open the casualty's air way and straighten their limbs – place two fingers under the casualty's chin and one hand on his forehead and gently tilt the head well back.

2. Straighten the casualty's limbs. (Make sure they have not suffered any broken bones first.)

3. Tuck the hand nearest to you, arm straight and palm upwards under the casualty's thigh.

4. Bring the furthermost arm from you across the casualty's chest. If you suspect that the casualty may have suffered a back or neck injury then you must make sure that their head and neck are supported at all times. Place the arm furthest from you over their chest and not under their cheek. If possible get someone else to help you put them in the recovery position so that you can support the head and neck.

5. Place the casualty's hand, palm outwards, against their cheek and, using your other hand, pull up the casualty's far leg just above the knee.

6. Keeping the casualty's hand pressed against his cheek, pull on the far leg and roll the casualty towards you until they are lying on their side.

7. Use your own body to prevent the casualty from rolling over too far and bend their upper leg at the knees so that it is at right angles to their body.

8. If necessary make any adjustments. It is important to recheck that the casualty's head is tilted well back in order to keep their airways open. Make sure that the casualty's lower arm is free and lying alongside their back with the palm facing upward.

A child aged between 1 and 7 should be placed in the same recovery position as an adult to prevent them from choking on their tongue or inhaling vomit.

A baby under the age of 12 months should be cradled in your arms with their head tilted downwards, again to prevent them from choking on their tongue or inhaling vomit.

To keep your child safe and to help you deal with any accidents or emergencies which may arise from time to time, parents would be advised to enrol on a basic first aid course.

◆ IMPORTANT ◆

When dealing with any accident or emergency situation always remain calm and follow the 'ABC' method:

A – **Airway** – Check the mouth for any obstructions

B – **Breathing** – Check for any signs of breathing

C – **Circulation** – Check for a pulse

If there is no response to breathing or circulation telephone 999 for an ambulance and commence mouth to mouth resuscitation (CPR) immediately. If you are in any doubt The Medical Dispatch Operator at the end of the telephone line will guide you through the procedure.

USEFUL TELEPHONE NUMBERS AND WEBSITES

Alcoholics Anonymous – 0345 697555

Barnardo's – 020 8550 8822 – www.barnardos.org.uk

Bullying UK – 020 7378 1446 – www.bullying.co.uk

Child Accident Prevention Trust (CAPT) – 020 7608 3828 – www.capt.org.uk

Childline – 0800 1111 – www.childline.co.uk

Drugs helpline – 0800 776600

Eating Disorders Association – 0845 634 7650 – www.edauk.com

Family Friends of Lesbian & Gays – 01454 852 418 – www.fflag.org.uk

Family Planning – 0845 310 1334 – www.fpa.org.uk

Information for Teenagers about Sex and Relationships – www.ruthinking.co.uk

Internet Watch Hotline – 0845 600 8844

Kidscape – 08451 205 204 – www.kidscape.org.uk

Message Home – 0800 700 740

Missing Persons – 0500 700 700 – www.missingpersons.org

National Aids helpline – 0800 567123

National Drugs Helpline (FRANK) – 0800 77 66 00 – www.talktofrank.com

NHS Direct – 0845 4647 – www.nhsdirect.nhs.uk

NSPCC – 0808 800 5000 – www.nspcc.org.uk

Royal Society for the Prevention of Accidents (RoSPA) – 0121 248 2000 – www.rospa.com

Samaritans – 0845 790 9090

Shelter – 0800 446441

Smokers Quitline – 0800 002200

Victim Support – 01702 333 911

Young Minds – 020 7336 8445 – www.youngminds.org.uk

Index

159